AF350021

Sadie Benning Suspended Animation

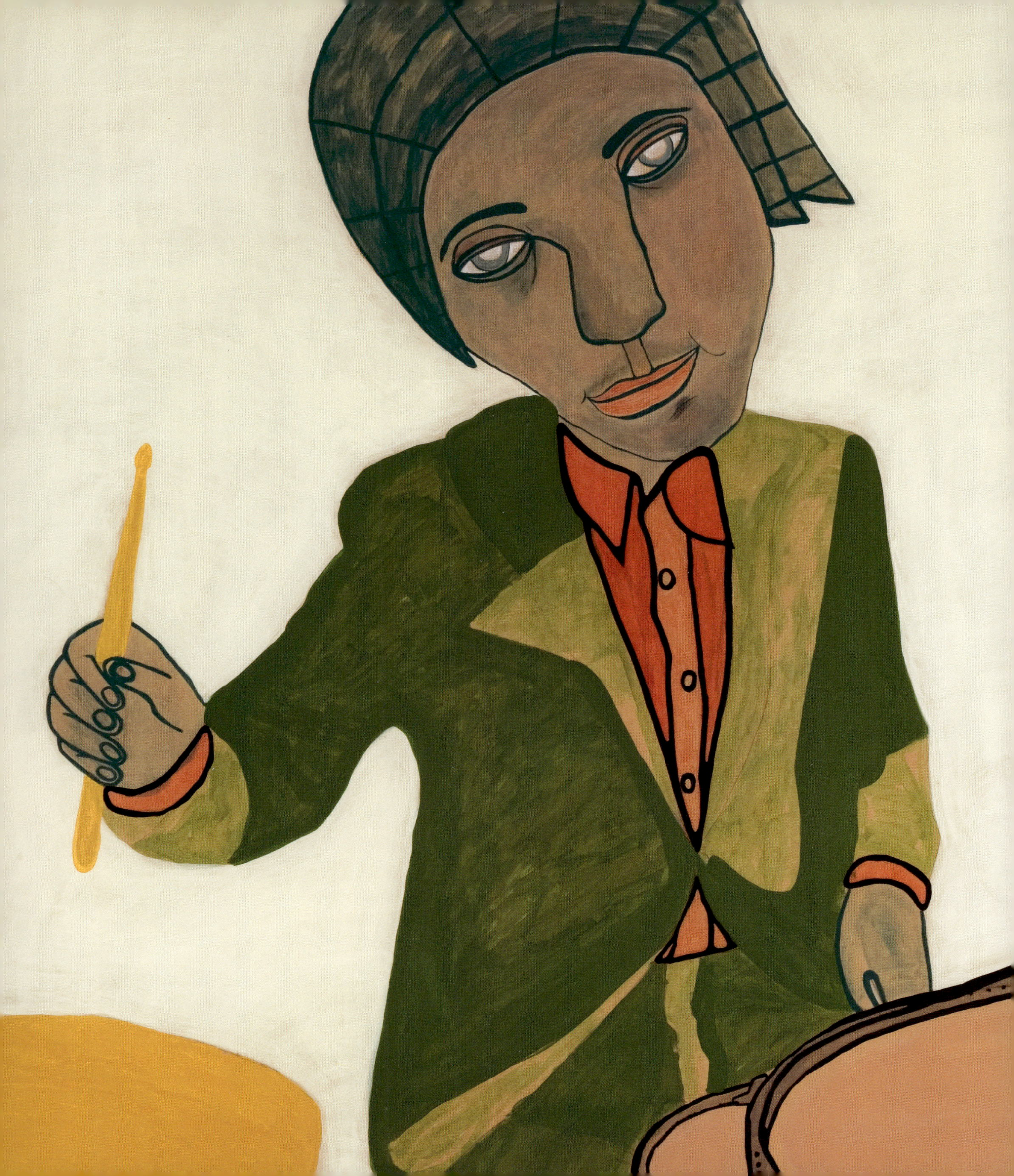

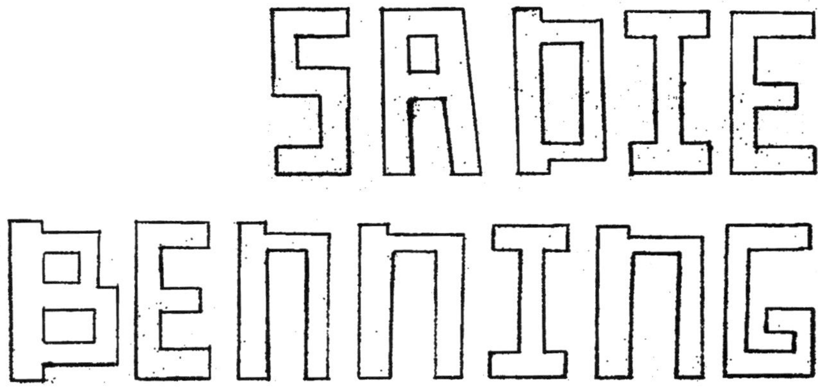

Suspended Animation

WEXNER CENTER FOR THE ARTS | THE OHIO STATE UNIVERSITY | COLUMBUS, OHIO | 2007

THIS PUBLICATION ACCOMPANIES THE EXHIBITION

Sadie Benning
Suspended Animation

Wexner Center for the Arts
The Ohio State University

January 26–April 15, 2007

CURATOR
Jennifer Lange

CATALOGUE EDITOR
Solveig Nelson

Suspended Animation was organized
by the Wexner Center for the Arts.

The exhibition is presented with
support from the Corporate Annual
Fund of the Wexner Center Foundation
and Wexner Center members.

PROJECT/EXHIBITION STAFF

CURATORIAL ASSISTANT
Nancy Schindele

GRAPHIC DESIGNER
M. Christopher Jones

EDITOR
Ann Bremner

© 2007
Wexner Center for the Arts
The Ohio State University

Library of Congress
Control Number: 2006939611

ISBN 10: 1-881390-41-1
ISBN 13: 978-1-881390-41-1

PUBLISHED BY
Wexner Center for the Arts
The Ohio State University
1871 North High Street
Columbus, Ohio 43210-1393
USA
Tel: +(614) 292-0330
Fax: +(614) 292-3369
www.wexarts.org

DISTRIBUTED BY
D.A.P. Distributed Art Publishers, Inc.
155 Sixth Avenue, 2nd Floor
New York, New York 10013
USA
Tel: +(212) 627-1999
         +(800) 338-2665
Fax: +(212) 627-9484
www.artbook.com

Front cover: assemblage from drawings for *Play Pause*.
End sheets and chapter frontispieces: details of drawings for *Play Pause*.
Photographs of paintings by Sadie Benning (pp. ii and 43–59) by Cory Piehowicz
for the Wexner Center for the Arts.

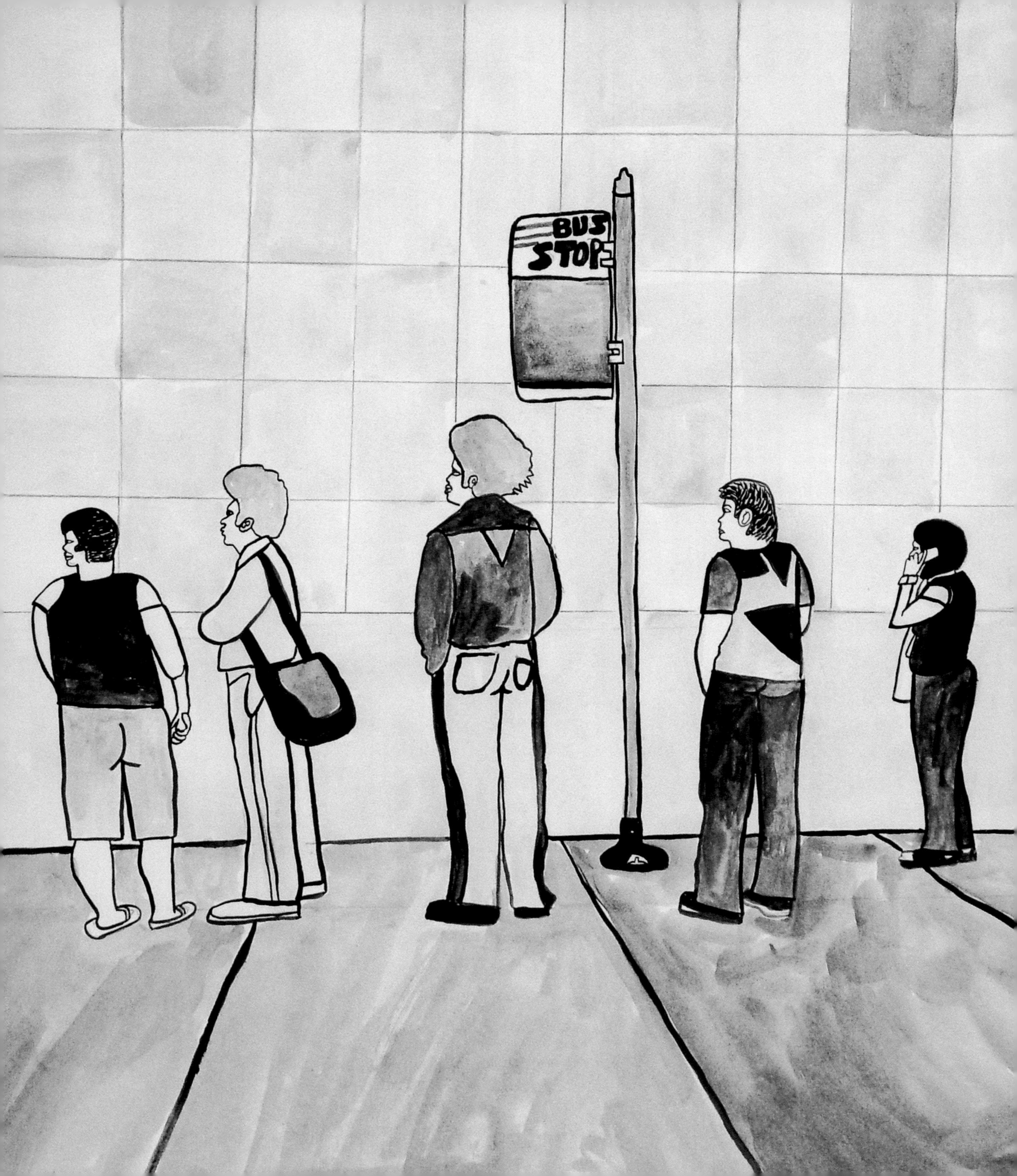

BUS
STOP

Given her own resolutely cross-disciplinary approach, Sadie Benning is an ideal subject of the Wexner Center's attentions, the perfect "fit" for a place where artistic explorations and migrations across all creative media consistently fuel the combustion of our multidisciplinary program. In *Suspended Animation*, Benning—best known for her work in video—exhibits large-scale paintings she has rarely shown before, and never in such abundance, along with *Play Pause*, an expansive new two-screen projection that is itself constructed from the artist's drawings. The Wexner Center is enormously pleased and proud to introduce these works to our gallery visitors and, through this catalogue, to a far larger audience of readers and viewers across the country and around the world.

The center's local audience initially encountered Benning's work back in October 1991, when several of her early Pixelvision videos were screened in an original series titled *Outcomes*. Benning herself first visited the center in 1998 to work in our Art & Technology (or Art & Tech) studio and editing suite, and several of her works were screened in a January 1999 series featuring artists who had participated in the Art & Tech program. She returned a few years later as the recipient of the 2003–04 Wexner Center Residency Award in media arts, and the center presented a retrospective series of her videos on that occasion. *The Baby*, one of two short works Benning completed during the residency, could well be seen as a precursor for *Play Pause*, especially in the way it uses the artist's drawings as a primary source activated by a kind of still, or suspended, animation.

As Jennifer Lange, the curator of *Suspended Animation*, relates in her introduction to this catalogue, the idea for the current exhibition also took shape during Benning's tenure as a residency artist. While plans for the show evolved over the next three years, the artist used Art & Tech as a production base for the development of *Play Pause*.

Now, with *Suspended Animation* installed in our galleries, Sadie Benning's work occupies a slightly different institutional position, one where our media arts and exhibitions programs intersect. From that perspective, her exhibition highlights the range of resources the Wexner Center can offer artists, in support of both the creation and the presentation of their work. The center's Art & Tech facility—unique in the nation—and its artists' residency program, which Jennifer describes more fully, vibrantly exemplify those resources. Art & Tech may well be largely hidden from public view, but it has become a beacon for media artists (and others). Film and video projects made with support from Art & Tech are frequently presented not only here at the center but at film/video festivals, museums, and other media venues internationally. Still, only those who routinely peruse the minutiae of film and video credits may register the fine print that typically acknowledges such support. And, since Art & Tech is not part of the Wexner Center's public spaces, visitors to our galleries or films or performances may not feel its hum of creative activity, except when visiting our relatively new video screening space, The Box.

That's one reason why we so enthusiastically embrace opportunities like this to showcase all that Art & Tech makes available to artists. Along with ample access to facilities, equipment, and expert staff assistance, the mere existence of a facility like Art & Tech provides artists encouragement—and permission—to explore new approaches or pursue projects of more extended scope or ambition than they might comfortably tackle on their own. Art & Tech is also the laboratory where many of the center's multidisciplinary and cross-disciplinary experiments are kindled and grow. Art & Tech residencies have supported the creation of dance pieces and galleries installations, as well as films and video works per se, and more than a few visual or performing artists have made their first forays into the realm of moving images under the program's auspices.

In *Play Pause*, which is at the center of the exhibition and woven visually into the very fabric of this catalogue, Benning moves the vector in another direction. She creates a new outlet for the practice of drawing that has long engaged her, and in doing so she sustains the lo-fi charm that gives her work such inimitable immediacy but, notably, through an art form—the installation of projected moving images—so often marked by high-tech polish.

The vibrantly colored paintings that surround the screening room for *Play Pause* similarly capture the idiosyncratic quirkiness of Benning's profoundly human (if ambiguously gendered) characters. As Helen Molesworth, the Wexner Center's chief curator of exhibitions, notes, they conjure up associations as varied as German expressionism and Olmec sculpture. Perhaps they form a Greek chorus for the pageant of contemporary urban life that unfolds in *Play Pause*, or maybe—as Benning and artist Amy Sillman discuss in the interview published here—they become its observers.

Certainly we at the Wexner Center have become observers and ardent admirers of Benning's work. The staff members, trustees, friends, volunteers, and other

associates involved in this exhibition and catalogue, as well as in Benning's residencies
at the center, form their own quite vivid roster of characters. Many are individually
recognized by Jennifer Lange in the acknowledgments that conclude her introduction.
I share her appreciation for their generous participation and join her in offering special
gratitude to our catalogue contributors: distinguished writers Eileen Myles and Aleksandar
Hemon; artist Amy Sillman, who joined Benning for a lively conversation; and editor
Solveig Nelson, who offered generous advice and assistance throughout the project.

Jennifer Lange, the center's associate curator of media arts, deserves considerable
recognition herself, for the grace and aplomb with which she orchestrated the diverse
dimensions of this project and its many creative collaborators. The entire media arts
department, under the direction of Bill Horrigan, has consistently provided moral
and professional support throughout Benning's longstanding relationship with the
Wexner Center. Helen Molesworth provided guidance and enthusiastic support from
the perspective of our exhibitions department, as well as a compelling and incisive
essay for this book, while Curatorial Assistant Nancy Schindele oversaw the countless
administrative and logistical details inherent in such a venture.

I would like to express my appreciation to the entire Board of Trustees and staff
of the Wexner Center for creating and sustaining an environment in which artists are free
to pursue multiple métiers: where they can delve, debate, digress, deviate, and dream.

Sherri Geldin

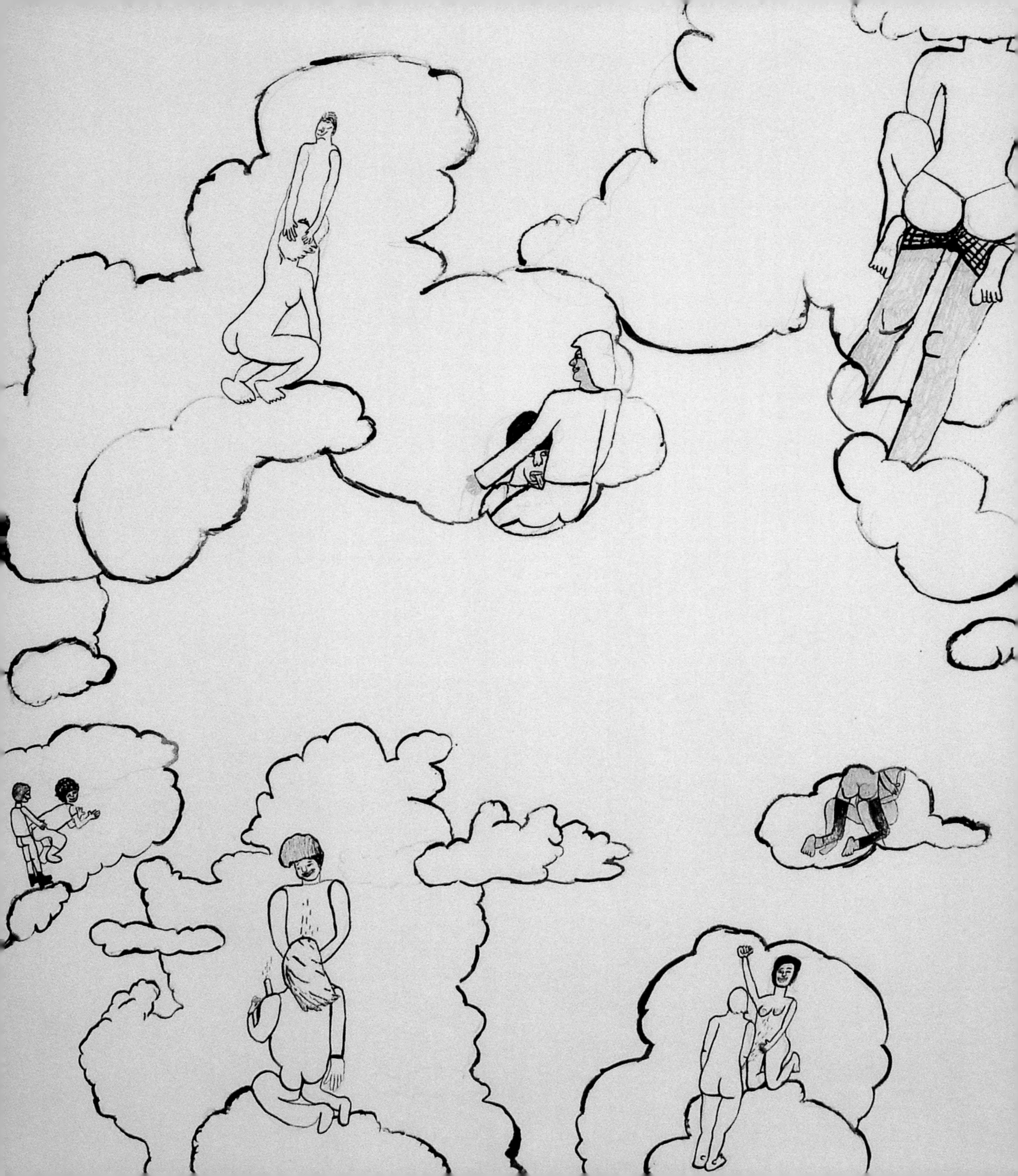

Jennifer Lange

Suspended Animation marks a number of firsts for Sadie Benning—her first solo gallery exhibition, the first public showing of her paintings as a sustained body of work, and her first two-channel video for gallery installation. It is quite fitting that all of this is happening at the Wexner Center, an institution that has vigorously supported her work over the past fifteen years and whose Art & Technology residency program has been a virtual second home to Sadie for the past three years.

It was in the spring of 2003 that I first called Sadie Benning to offer her our 2003–04 Wexner Center Residency Award in media arts. I remember that we talked for a long time for people who didn't know each other, and that we did so with a certain familiarity, like old friends almost, that was unexpected and disarming. That initial conversation, during which she revealed that she had been filling her studio with large and colorful painted portraits only a handful of people had yet seen, planted a seed in both our minds that would eventually grow into *Suspended Animation*. At that time, the idea for the *Play Pause* video was just that—an idea whose starting point was some "sex drawings" that Sadie had been making for the past few years.

As curator of the Art & Technology residency program (Art & Tech, for short), I am in the unique and enviable position of witnessing firsthand the creative process of our visiting artists. Every year fifteen to twenty artists come from around the world to work in Art & Tech on the production and/or postproduction of their videos and films. With three digital editing systems comparable to those found in commercial facilities, a sizable studio outfitted with production equipment, and a staff with the enthusiasm and technical skills to try just about anything, there is very little that we can't do. The program is unique in that we ask artists for very little in return: credit on the work, a copy for our archive, and the opportunity to show the work. With this level of freedom, and with an invitation to stay in residence for as long as necessary, artists are able to experiment and to refine their vision. Works supported by the program range from documentaries to video installations to experimental short works.

Sadie embodies the freedom and uniqueness of the Art & Tech program—all that our program can do for an artist. Often staying for months at a time, she would arrive armed with drawings, cameras, and boxes of supplies—items that quickly decorated and defined the studio space. Once ensconced, Sadie's process began: shooting, drawing, reshooting, editing, recording sound, making music. Witnessing the evolution of *Play Pause* over the past three years has been a remarkable and gratifying experience. For me, music and sound have always seemed integral to the work—to all of Sadie's work, really—and some of my fondest memories of Sadie's visits are of the music, both the music she made for *Play Pause* and the music she listened to while shooting the hundreds of drawings created for the video. Her music—often set to repeat endlessly—would echo throughout the studios, providing a soundtrack for the day.

This exhibition could not have been realized without the support, advice, and friendship of Art & Tech editors Paul Hill and Mike Olenick, both of whom worked with Sadie. Their talents and skills are often hidden behind the vision of the artists with whom they work, but without them those visions would not be realized. *Suspended Animation* was originally conceived of in collaboration with Claudine Isé, my former colleague in the Wexner Center's exhibitions department. Her enthusiasm and leadership provided the foundation for the exhibition. The extraordinary vision of Bill Horrigan, director of the media arts department, shaped the Art & Tech program, and he has been a constant source of support and advice in the planning of this exhibition. Chief Curator of Exhibitions Helen Molesworth ensured the exhibition's success with her consistent guidance and good humor and, of course, with her contribution of an insightful essay to this catalogue. I am also grateful to Eileen Myles, Aleksandar Hemon, and Amy Sillman for their contributions to the catalogue; each piece—two essays and a conversation with the artist—has a distinctive style that helps us understand Sadie's work from a fresh and thoughtful perspective. In addition to collaborating with Sadie on *Play Pause*, Solveig Nelson deserves enormous thanks for her work on this catalogue and assistance in organizing the exhibition.

I am grateful to all my colleagues at the Wexner Center for their support of Sadie and this exhibition, especially Jonathan Achor, Ann Bremner, Jill Davis, Erin Donavan, Portia Edwards, Dave Filipi, Will Fugman, Larry Heller, Chris Jones, Steve Jones, David Kasprzak, Kevin Lenander, Megan Cavanaugh Novak, Ryan Osborne, Nancy Schindele, Chris Stults, and Mike Sullivan. Director Sherri Geldin has always been a steadfast supporter of the Art & Tech program and has warmly welcomed Sadie to the Wexner Center over the years.

And lastly, thanks to Sadie Benning for infusing Art & Tech—and the entire Wexner Center—with her magnetic personality, sense of humor, and vision. It is a thrill to be the first institution to present this body of work to the public.

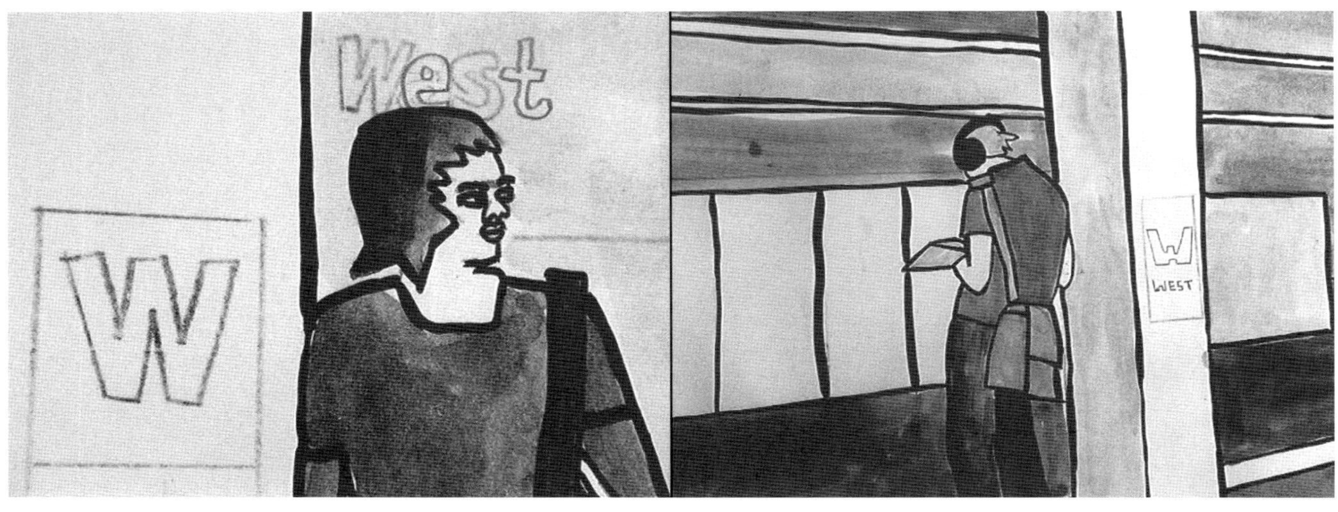
West
W
W
WEST

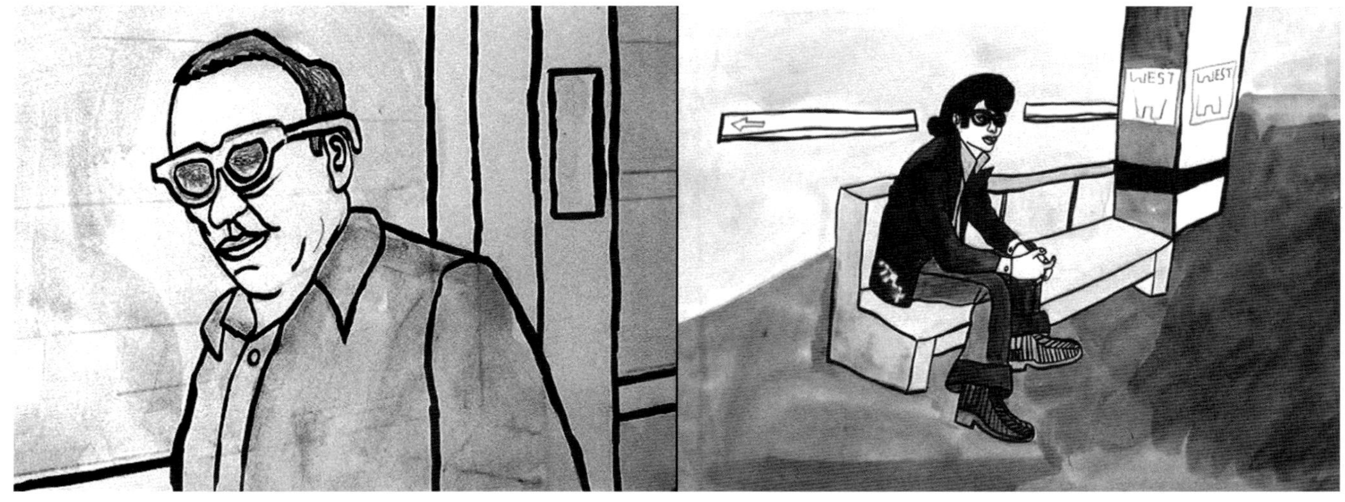WEST
WEST

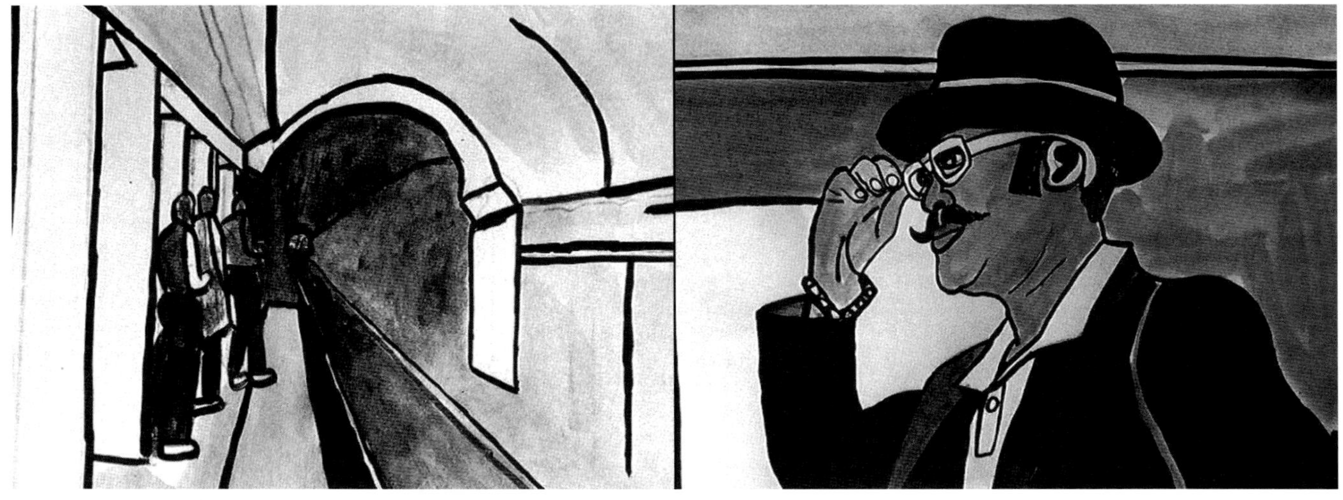

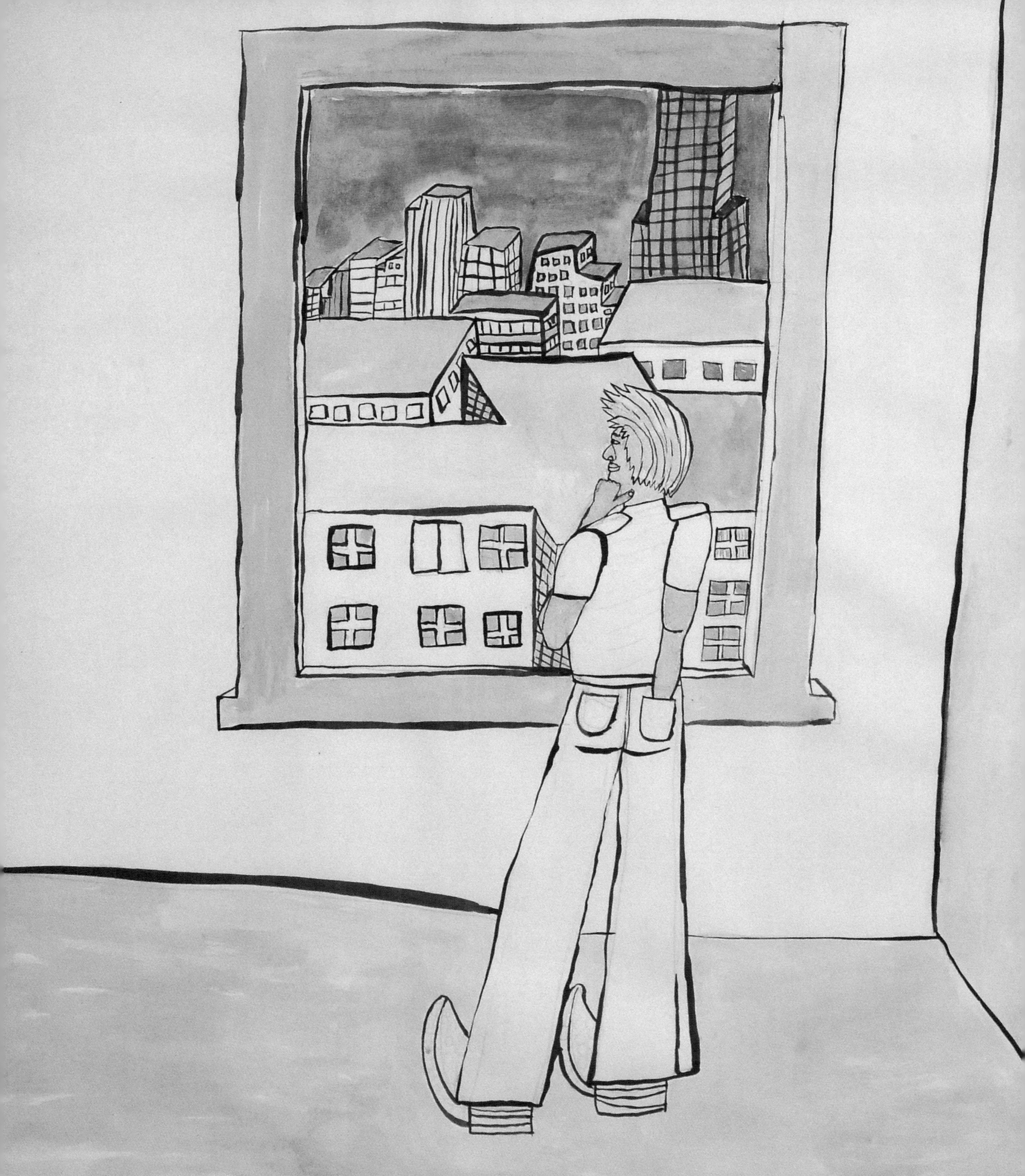

Eileen Myles

I kind of acted like a gross guy with Sadie's new video. Trotted it around like the new girl in tow. So of course I even did watch it in bed with the new girl and (how guy of me is this?) she's *so* much smarter than I am. She used a lot of field recordings, said Paige quietly. Field recordings? What's that?

By the time I got back to California I was having dinner with Susan and Darwin and Taylor, friends of mine who happen to be a nuclear family. I figured they would have a whole other perspective on Sadie. Stupidly I told them I was writing about her video, so anything you say might wind up in my piece. That was real brilliant of me. They promptly shut up.

There's a lot of sex—gay sex—in *Play Pause*. I keep wanting to call it *Play Paws*. Because it's fun. If you look at all of Sadie's work in a great rush you begin to see that her earliest videos are like comic books. Or circus. The bold kid titles for each little video: pure cartoon. The scribbled ransom-note dialogue is like cartoon bubbles, but torn instead of drawn and stuck on the inside of her film. Cough, I mean video.

Anyhow I'm watching *Play Pause* with my family and prior to this viewing I had been entirely approving of how Sadie scattered moments not so much of pussy-eating or fucking but of *about to* (pussy-eat or fuck) throughout her video. I've been kind of obsessed for a few years now with this thing Robert Smithson liked, an idea which *he* lifted from an anthropologist, Anton Ehrenweig, that cultures can generally be divided

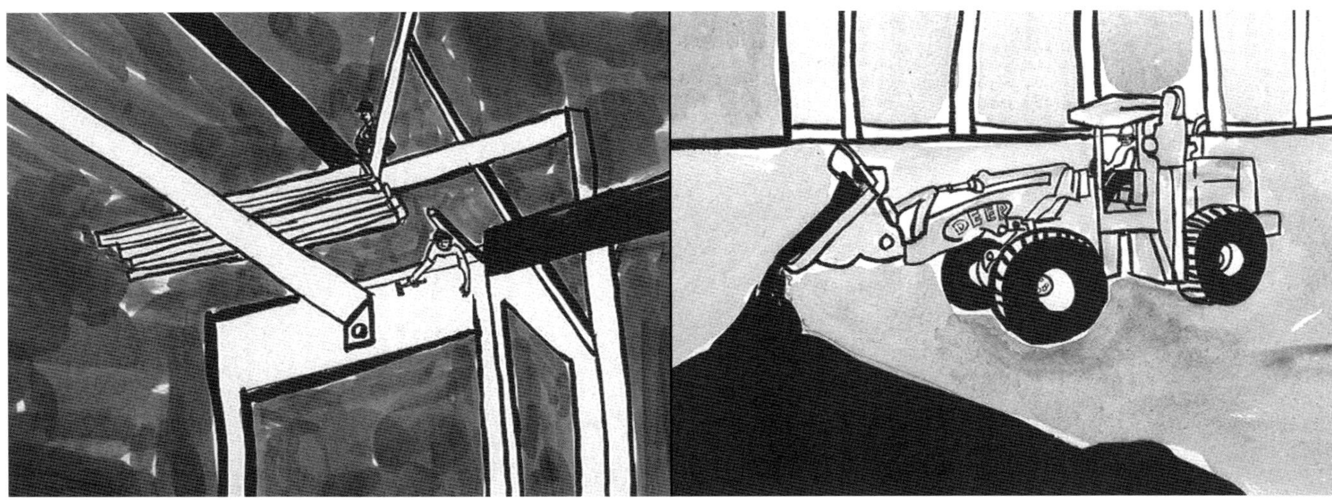

into two types—ones with a buried god, and the ones with a strewn one. I'm thinking about sex here in place of god, and in the case of Sadie thinking that though there are artists who might actually bury their sexual content in their work (like a dog buries a bone), other artists let the sex be strewn throughout their productions. Of course all in vastly different proportions. The thing about gay content is that it's so often strewn instead of buried because you know if it's buried then you wind up in a don't ask don't tell kind of situation. It's the straight way of being gay, pretty much, and of course what's implied by that approach is a whole lot of invisible power, i.e., I think that only the implicitly powerful can readily bury their sex or their gods and not feel somewhat erased themselves as a result.

Lesbian content always pretty much has to be visible; that's how it goes. But Sadie's distribution of the item seemed to me to be on the order of like lesbian ripple or chip. A lesbian ice cream *flavor* pretty much, rather than you know head-on lesbian shit and so on.

But when I watched it with my family, well.

It was just kind of still. These are hip people but I know everyone was thinking is it okay for me to be watching this with my kid, my parents, my friend. That quiet thought was cycling through the room. I went ha-rumph. *My friend* (I meant Paige) described these as field recordings. That's interesting, said Darwin who is a scientist. For *us* pretty much anything done outside of the laboratory is in the field. Which is the world. And then I think well this work of Sadie's, this extremely I think allegorical cartoon of this phenomenal moment we are all living in, is a fairly scientific work. Though geeky play science. Also like Smithson! Certainly Sadie rides her bike around Chicago or wherever, this generic depressed fertile Midwestern city, and obviously for some of that time she's traveling around with a tape recorder like Alan Lomax. Getting a folk recording of the world. How it was. Sadie tells me that she started with the sex,

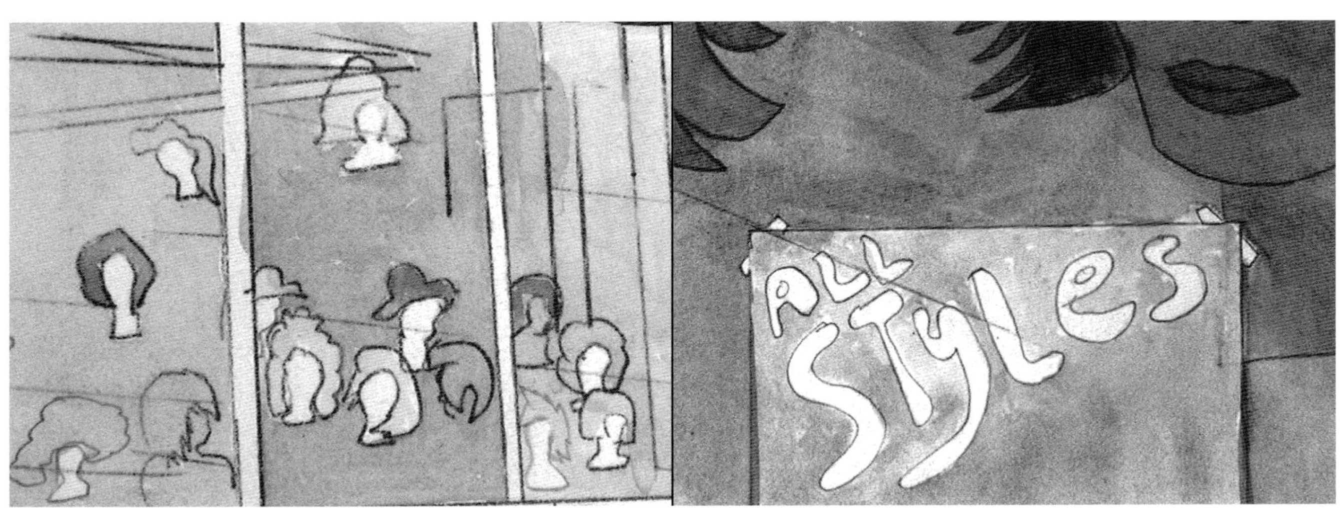

which is so funny. She drew it first. I thought it was strewn, erupting every once in a while like a huffy little volcano. But when I watched it with my friends I was actually closer to the truth—of the piece. Sadie built a world around the real and imagined sex—the inside of the world that we know. She constructed a tiny town. But sex is the train. The game. The reason. Everyone has sex, even if they don't. She pointed out to me that it was kind of generic sex. Afterwards or before. The sex is actually never happening. People are exposed, ready or else spent. And so she was thinking that that makes the sex a little more universal perhaps. She didn't use that word, but I think she meant user-friendly. It's like the sex pushed *Play Pause* like the sex was kind of god. And God says, Hey Honey I'm going to go out and get some cigarettes, maybe something for us to drink, but you know since there aren't any stores or other people or bars, I'm going to have to make them so it might take a little while. So I think this is a video generated by an act of love about to happen. And the skies came first too. Those strange sifting metal sculpture skies. I think about sitting on a plane in one of those wonderful composed moods you get flying. I look up and the what do you call it, the fin of the plane, had a raccoon. Look there's a raccoon out there, I said to no one into my little microphone probably in a poem. Sadie has some people having sex on the fin. No this is not subtle, this is a couple actually fucking. Let me look again. In one of Sadie's earlier films the entire screen gets filled by a fish. Just swimming around in the water. It was perfect. Films are wishful, aren't they. It's just a wish floating around. A gay teen decides to stay home from school and make her *own* world. I told Sadie about how the most famous people I knew in New York, Allen Ginsberg and Andy Warhol, always went around with a camera. I'm looking at you buddy. That's what's going on here. Everyone was staring at Sadie when she was a kid. Trying to figure out what sex she was. So she just went and made her own fameful representation. Initially she kind of joined the staring people and her camera was staring at her but

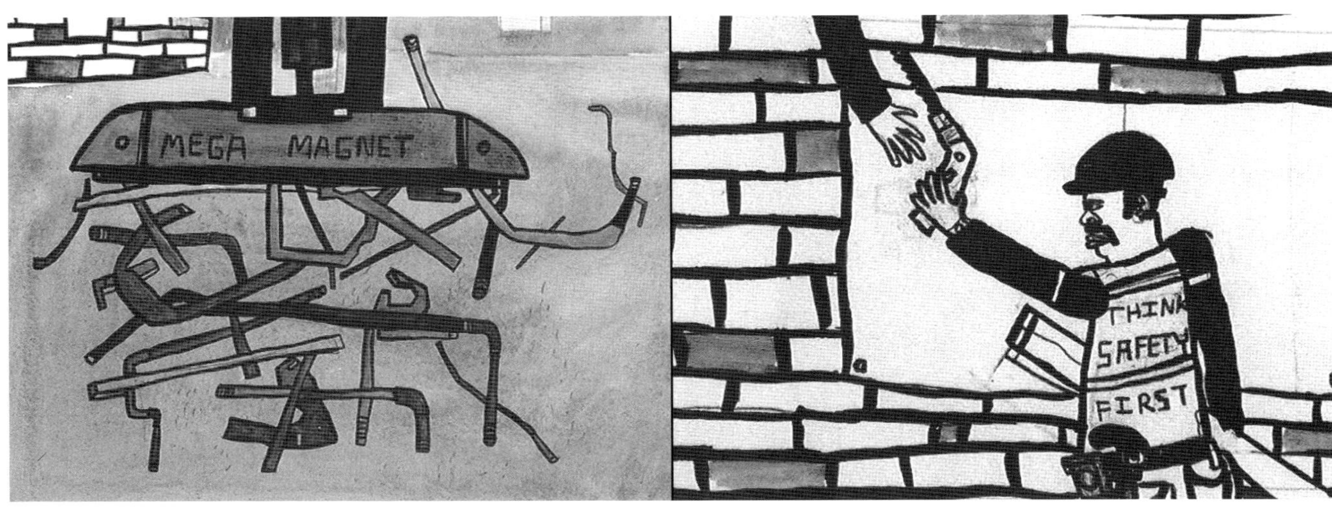

then it started moving around, and slowly she began to replace herself. I notice in her films that when her face is talking there's no mouth on the screen. So to me the film was all mouth. Like the missing mouth was the film's moons. Its rings. And later she made masks. And a pencil drawing, a line. Soon the world was drawings on walls, signs on stores, and stores that were closed, just signs. That's a real depressed city. Ads selling things that weren't there. Remember when the world became an ad for the web. Around 1998 I think. It was great but it was hard to know anymore which world came first. Then eventually Sadie was gone. In her work. No Sadie to be found. But wasn't Sadie *always* a mask.

I drove my truck to the beach last week. I'm in San Diego. The beach is everywhere here. I sat in my truck with my computer on my lap and I pushed the button (well the picture of a button on the screen) and I watched *Play Pause* surrounded by the gleaming ocean with streams of late afternoon light jumping around on it. A film is an ocean, right. This is real, *and* this is real. The setting was perfect. Balanced. Some people think the world stopped a few years ago. Certainly that world that we know is gone. It seems to me that when I look at all of Sadie's work she's always taking something away to make everything else move. Someone said that this video is sad. And it is. Listen to the music at the beginning while the train rattles by in our eyes. And then there was sex and she put the world back and probably we can have everything when we're ready. If we know what to push.

MAY 29, 2006

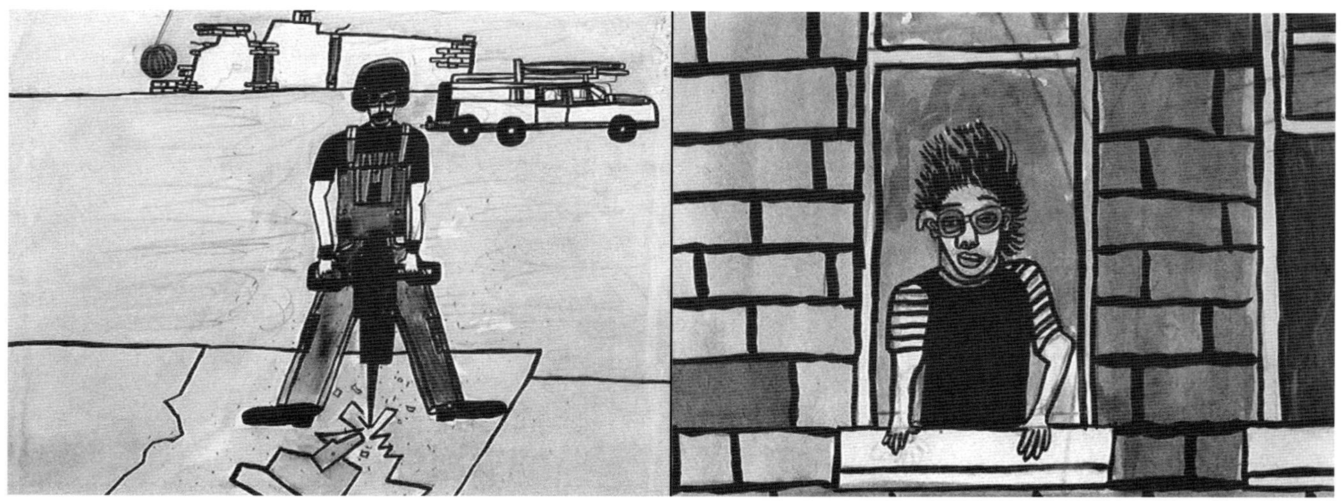

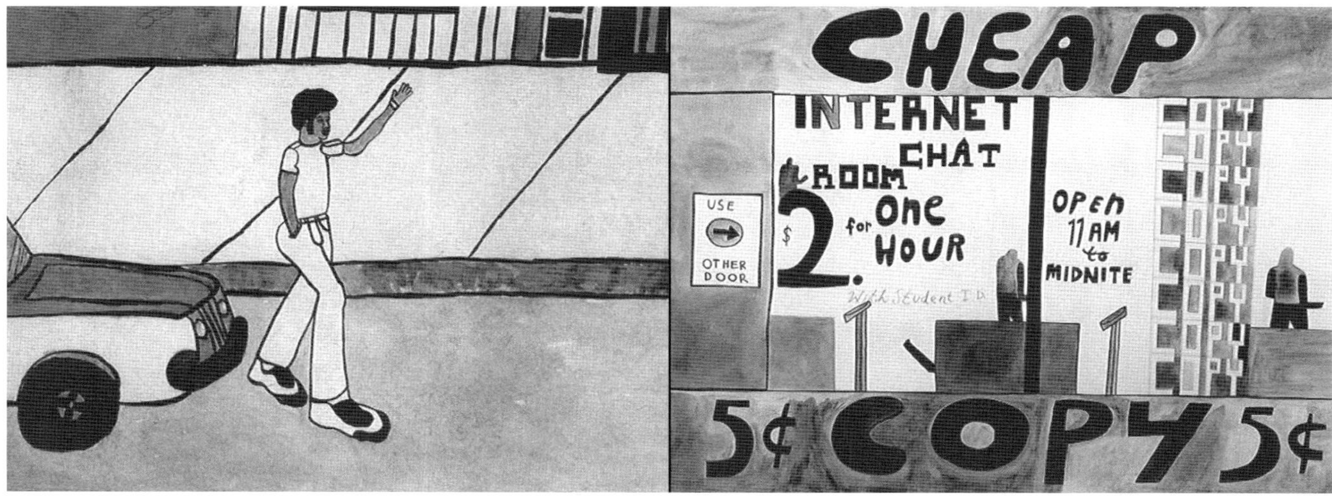
CHEAP
INTERNET
CHAT
ROOM
$2. for ONE HOUR
With Student I.D.
USE
OTHER
DOOR
OPEN
11 AM
to
MIDNITE
5¢ COPY 5¢

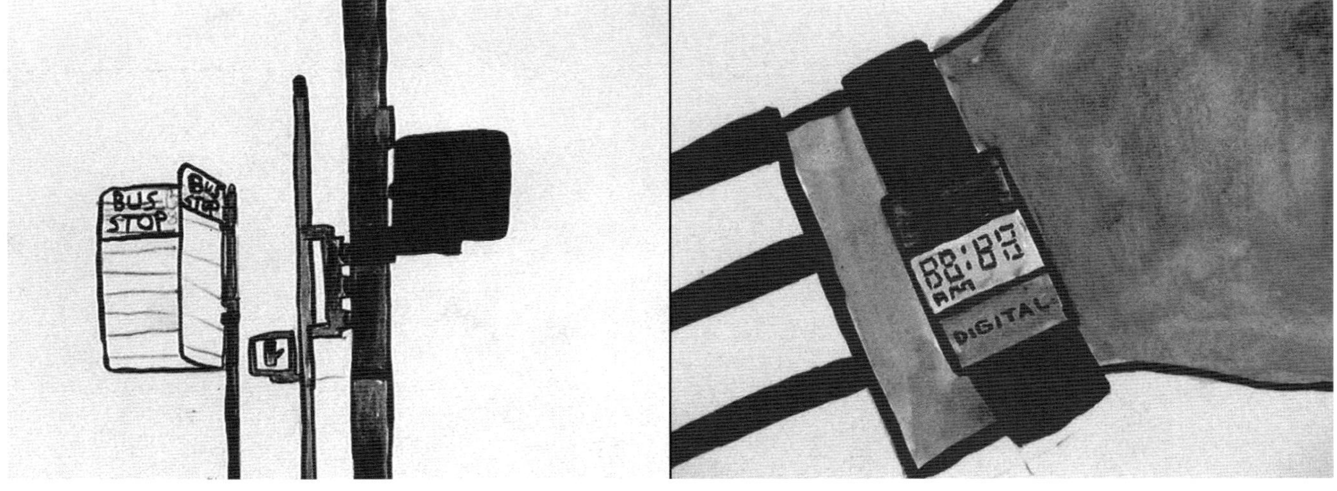
BUS
STOP
BUS
STOP
88:88
AM
DIGITAL

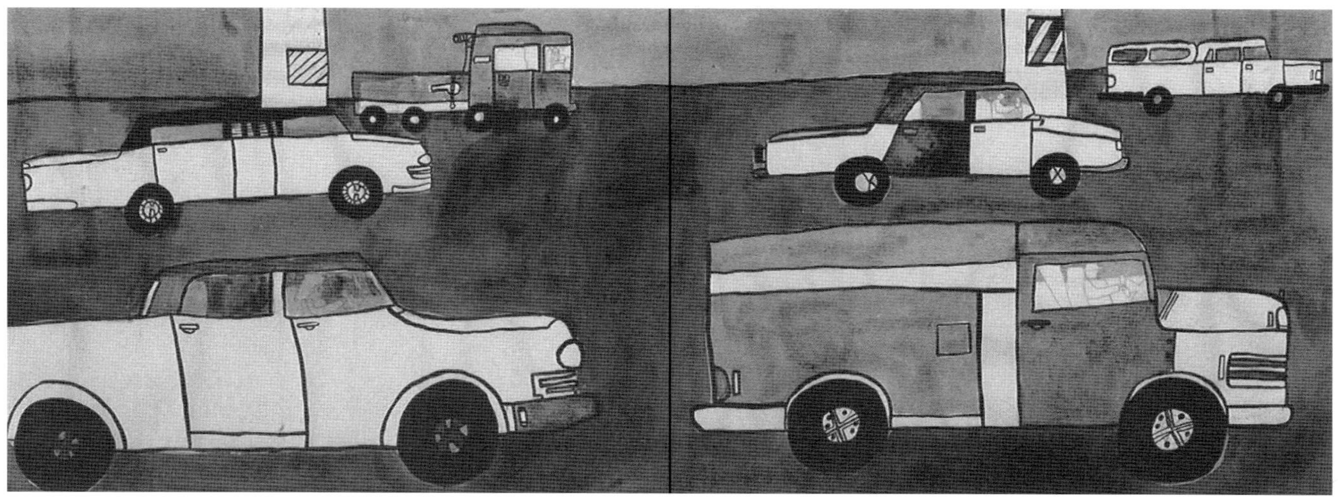

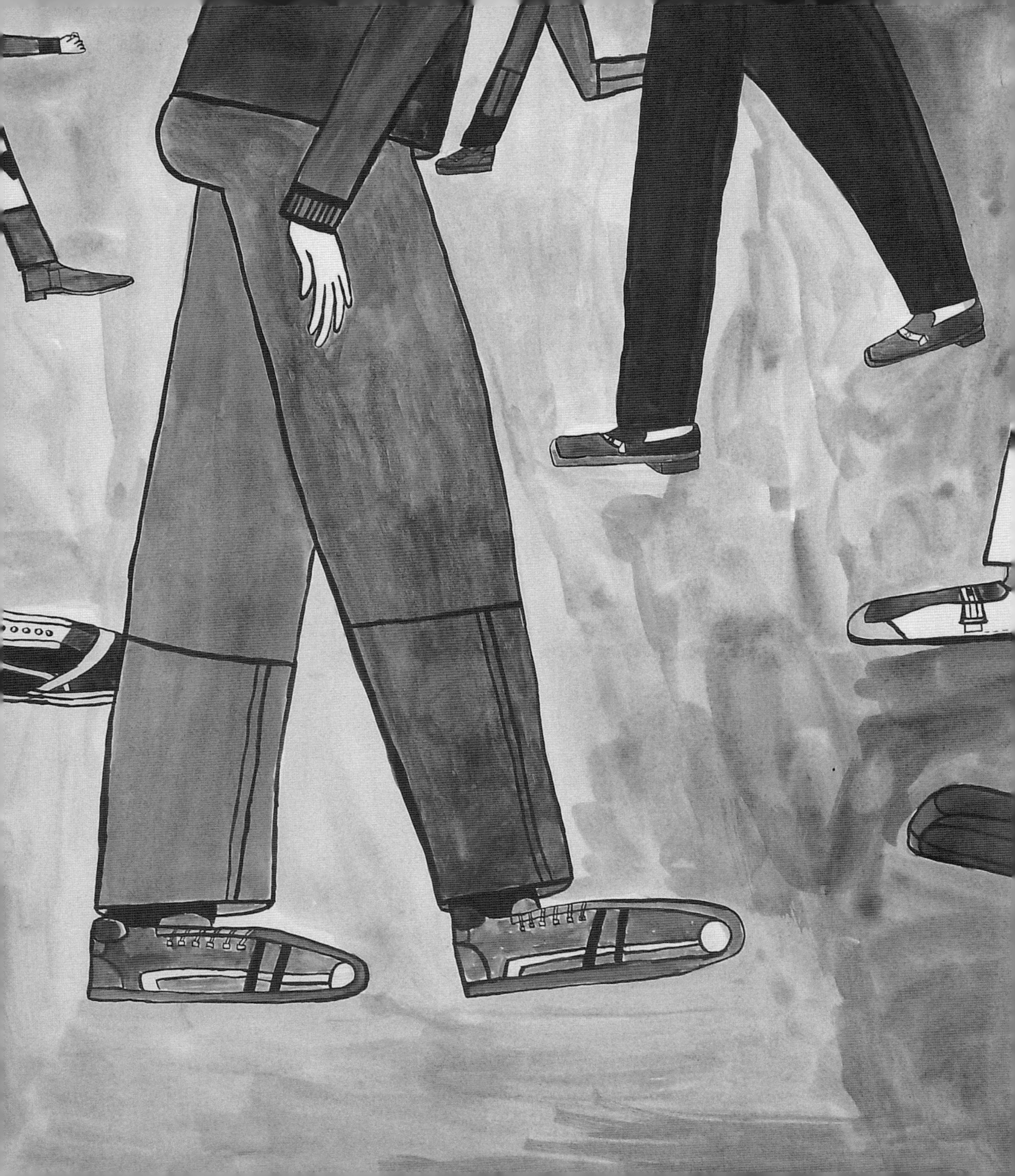

AMY SILLMAN   Do you see *Play Pause* as an installation, something people can walk into anywhere?

SADIE BENNING   I think they will. I do see the video as having a linear order, even though it's fragmented and there is no main character. Maybe the viewer could partially be a character because I'm constructing it in a way where I want them to be witnessing all of these moments.

AS   The first part of *Play Pause* seems to be about a citizen of a city walking through the streets, but it's also a very poetic space where people are all absorbed into their own thoughts. Maybe they're reading or waiting for the train or trying to get money out of the ATM, or watching other people do those things, but consciousness is all over the place. And later on the video becomes more subsumed with the spectacle of longing. It gets really flirtatious and sexy and actually becomes sex, but in a funny way that makes you drag yourself away from the private subjectivity that is the beginning.

SB   I think maybe there is something intrinsic to being queer in the world where there's a kind of loneliness to some degree, in that you don't always have

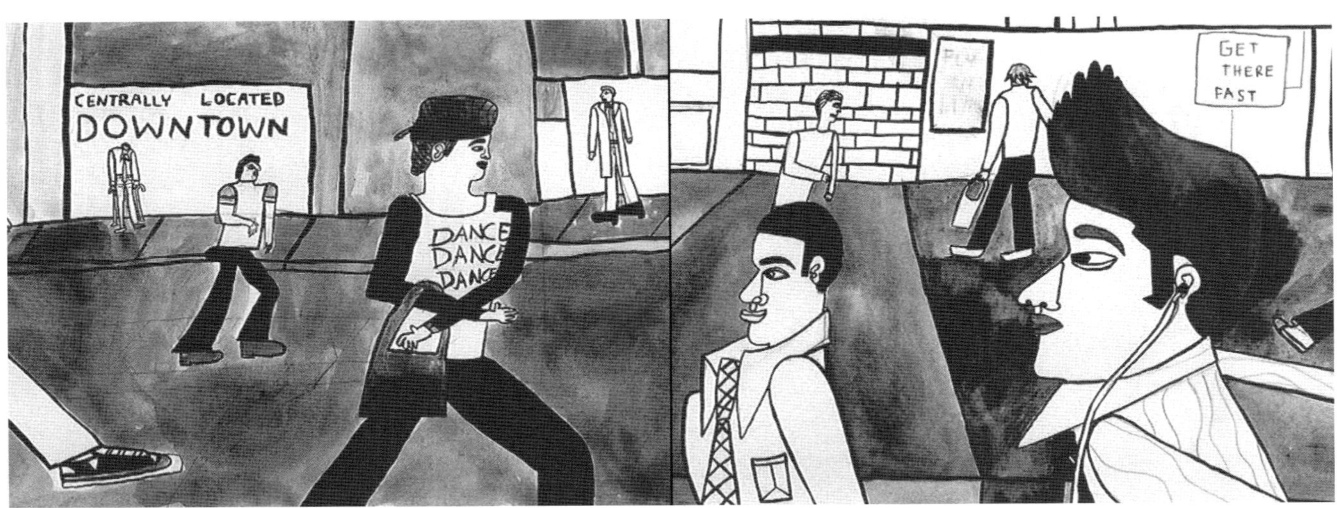

things to identify with. You're looking for those things in signs and in more transitory glances.

AS   Like wig stores that don't really capture your look (laughs)—

SB   Or maybe they do (laughs).… I think that I'm always looking for things that are really different from myself when I'm out in the world. But I'm also looking for affirmation that my reality is not totally insane, particularly in the political environment right now.

AS   Is *Play Pause* based on stuff that has happened to you?

SB   (laughs) Well, definitely it's about observing the space around me. And the soundtrack was created from hours of ambient recordings I made in Chicago and Milwaukee. I started *Play Pause* soon after September 11th, and I was thinking a lot about cities and how I felt suspended in this moment where you're not exactly sure what's going to happen. So I wanted to aesthetically capture that feeling of being frozen rather than animating everything. The piece is constructed almost entirely out of still-frame imagery.

AS   What's the reason?

SB   When something traumatic happens it's like being paused at that moment, so everything is kind of post-9/11 now. There's this marker in time.

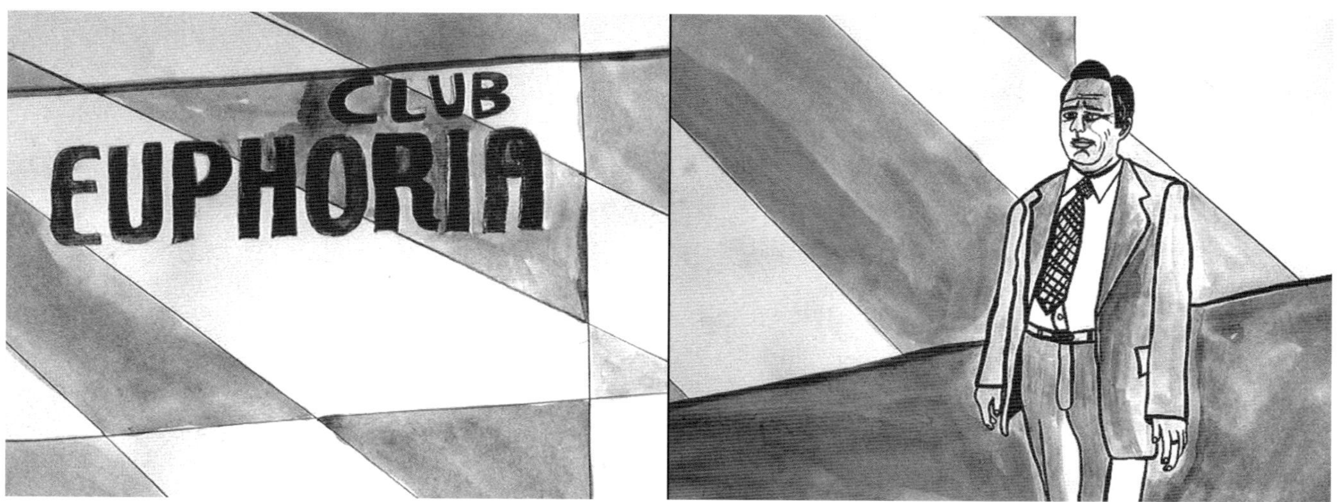

AS   And trauma changes your notion of time. Trauma makes you feel that maybe there's a super consciousness, and in editing *Play Pause* as a double-screen projection where things are fading and splitting and never held to one consistent temporal reality, you're emphasizing the trauma of everyday life.

SB   Right, and I think it's also connected to gender and sexuality. Somehow initially when I was figuring out my own sexuality, I didn't know any lesbians—I only knew gay men. My mom's best friend lived with us, and he became HIV positive around 1989. So as a child I identified with the idea that queer sexuality was connected to loss. ACT UP was a big part of my growing up. More recently when I first started thinking about making the video and wanting it to have a certain emotional quality, I was going through a period of personal grief. If somebody dies you have a heightened sense of your surroundings, or at least I did. It was like, oh, turn off the radio or whatever—you just think things are loud or everything seems brighter. You're more sensitive, and you're looking for signs of that person in all of these objects. There's a kind of otherness present if somebody dies.

AS   I first saw *Play Pause* as realism in the city, and then as a kind of fantasy with sexuality. Now I'm seeing it more the way you're talking about it. You're bringing up two parallel traumas in America—the beginning of the AIDS crisis, when trauma became associated with sex, and 9/11, when trauma became associated with urban life. You're not saying that they're the same thing, but images of the city, images of gay bars, images that are generally in this film have double meanings.

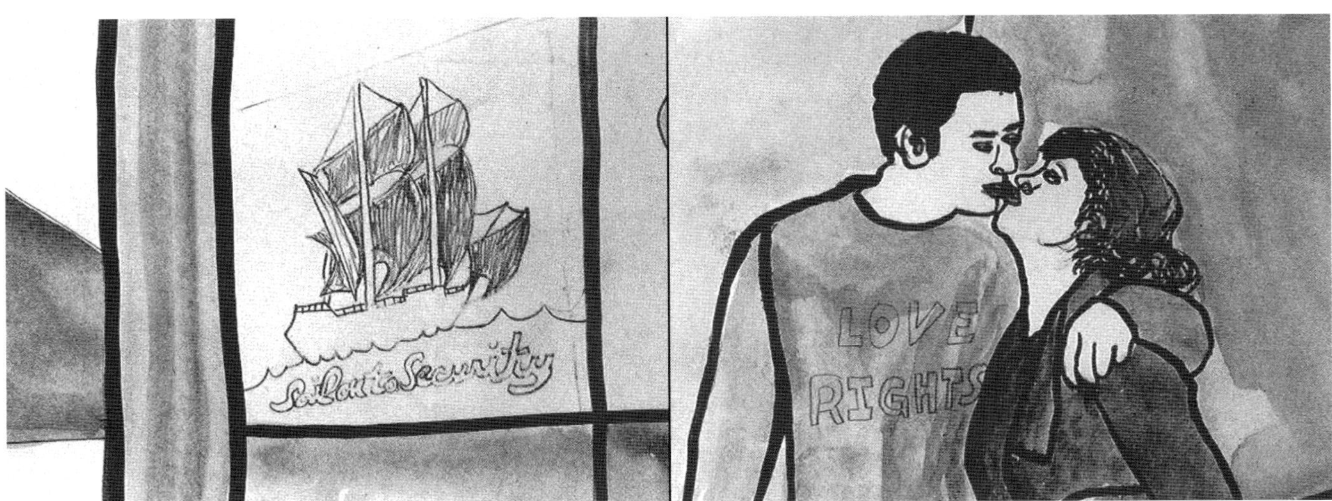

SB   I wanted to make something that was more about the ambient experience of loss rather than showing it literally. That's why there aren't any direct references to September 11th and it doesn't take place in New York. It's hard to know what city or time period it takes place in exactly. The video is based in the present, but it's about the way that you're constantly reminded of other places and times.

AS   You said yesterday that *Play Pause* started as two separate projects?

SB   I was working on drawings of sexual experiences that are more awkward or in-between than what I usually see represented—for example before or after somebody's had sex, or maybe there's another kind of connection happening. I had also been developing a more narrative work about a city, and those two projects merged together.

AS   The piece seems to take place after something happened which is never specified, but which we all relate to in an "after" kind of way. The experience described in the beginning of *Play Pause* is that of coming back to life. You're not in bed totally depressed and grief-stricken. You're starting to look around, but with a sense of detachment.

SB   I think that in those moments people want euphoria, and sex is often something that does that. The video is also about connecting

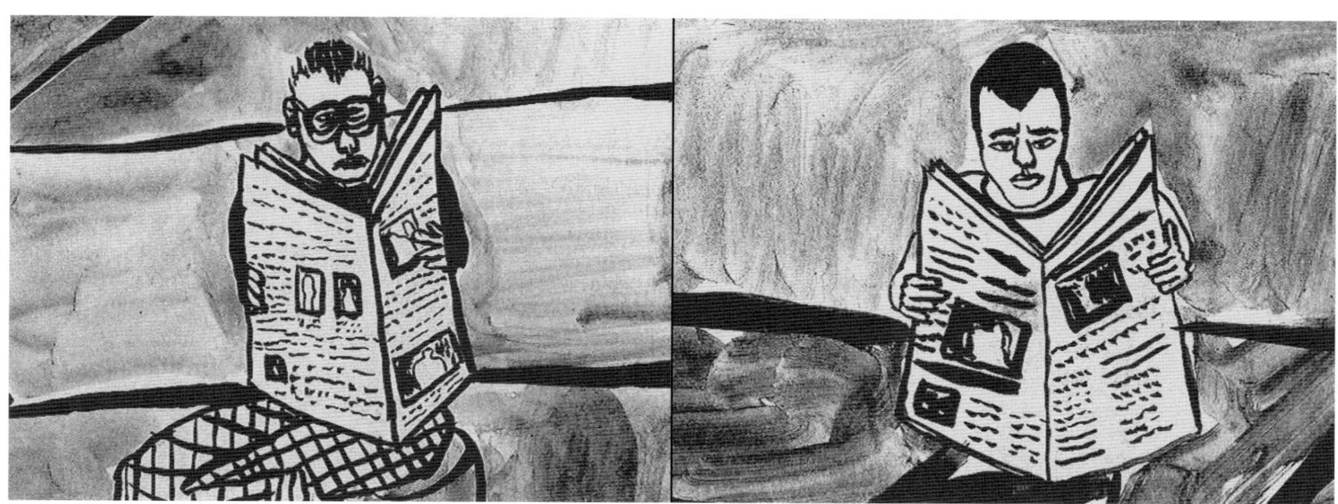

with a more intuitive space, one that's more abstract and about just looking—

AS   Or even patterns—

SB   Yeah, the pattern of the leaves or whatever. There's something really important about that kind of abstraction. For example, I think that even when I draw characters who are having sex, I don't know exactly what gender they are or how they identify. I mean, it's a drawing (laughs). Which is I think why portraits or heads are interesting to me, because it's a part of the body that is so detached. Like it's the face and it's narrative, but it's not necessarily male or female; it's more a space of expressions that's not so specific to gender.

AS   One thing that's interesting is that the drawing changes as you draw it, so the person could be a female when you draw their hair, and a male by the time you draw their feet. So if the whole video is built on a series of drawings that themselves are uncertain about their outcome, it's recording aspects of something that didn't know what it was.

SB   Right, which is a form of animation even though it ends up as a still drawing. It's coming out of this imagined space that's moving as you're making it.

AS   And furthermore, the cutting and the detailing and the fragmenting of the video make it even more unclear, or rest strongly on the more

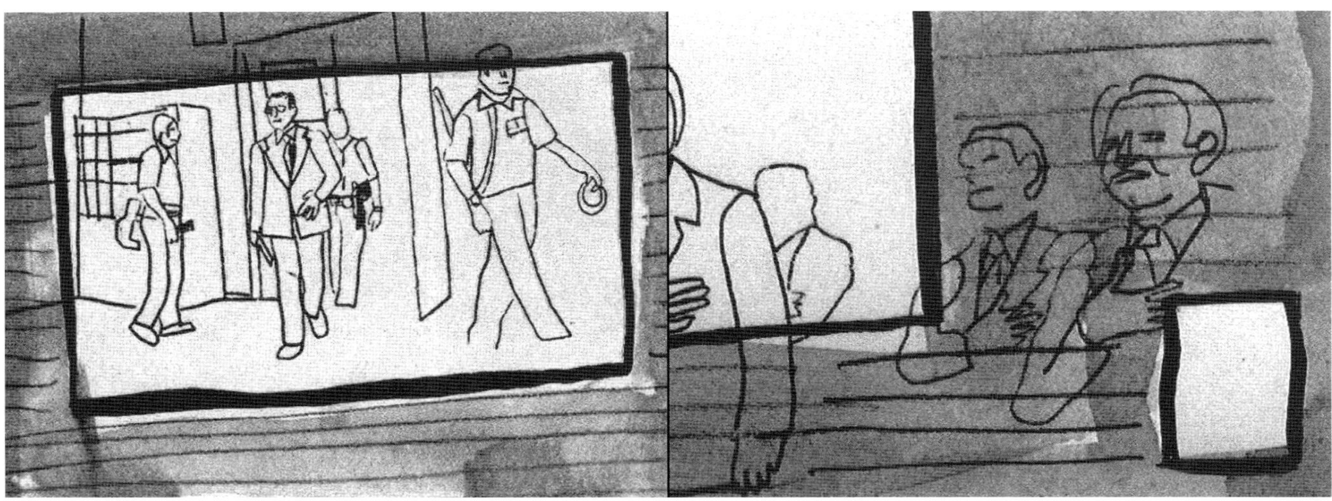

ambiguous parts of the original drawings; because if you have a close-up of two policemen's crotches, we still don't know whether they have wigs on.

SB   Right (laughs). I mean some of the drawings in *Play Pause* use a technique of blowing up and tracing photographs that comes from having visited Henry Darger's apartment and looking closely at his process.

AS   There's a scene of mannequin heads that has a very Henry Darger feeling to it—

SB   It's more about pencil. The line has a more tentative quality.

AS   Those parts are really important formally because they interweave with the way that the outline that you do is often very heavy. It reminds me of Saul Steinberg, or you've talked about the influence of the *Plains Indians Drawings* exhibition at the Drawing Center. But in all pictographic drawing, the outline is the crucial thing.

SB   I think that partially comes from having used the Pixelvision camera for such a long time. The contrast in Pixel is so extreme it makes things seem as if they're outlined; if you have your hand up, it's going to silhouette everything. And because of the blockiness of Pixel and how much less information there is, the image becomes more abstracted somehow. The thing with Pixel is you can't use that camera forever because it's a toy, and it's going to die. One of the reasons I started drawing was out of a complete frustration with technology. My equipment kept breaking, and the thing that made me feel

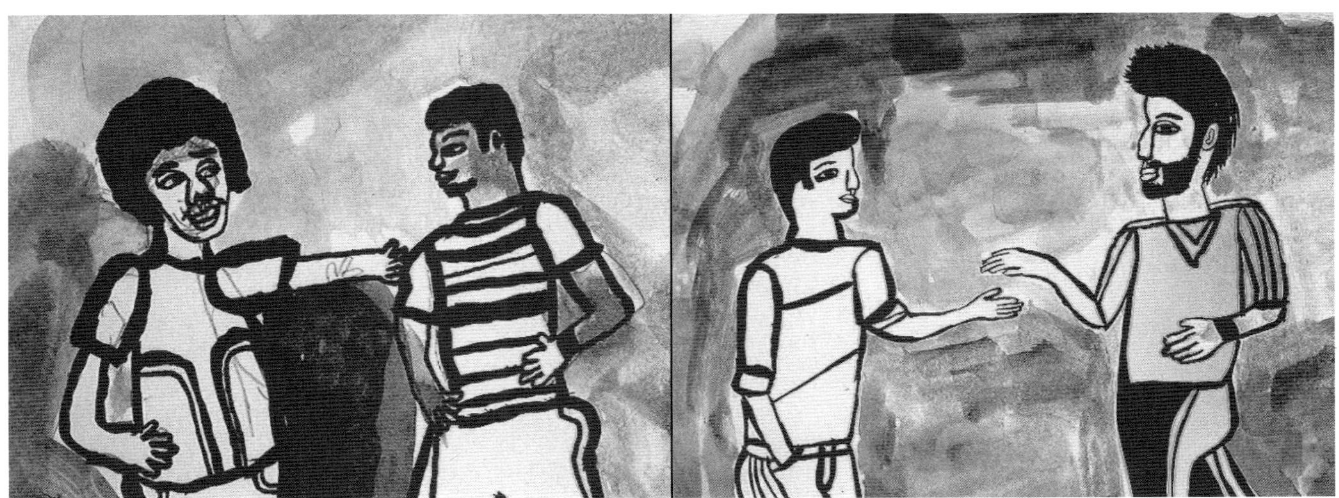

better was I could go and paint or draw something. Then also with drawing I wanted to emulate things I liked about the xeroxed, dreamlike quality of Pixelvision. Shooting the drawings on video is the closest I can come to that reality.

AS   I think this is important because drawing as a medium asserts the primacy of a very malleable, imagination-driven version of reality. Because drawing is like transcribing a combination of realities, from what is imagined to what is seen. And there's this thing about flatness, too. Your work resolutely holds to a flat space and then does everything it can to take that flat space and temporalize it rather than spatialize it. *Play Pause* is very much about before and after and building moments.

SB   It's also like vision, the way that you blink and you look and you turn. It has this shuttered on and off rhythm.

AS   The piece is kind of a record of both looking and not looking. It feels like one has one's eyes closed half the time. And sometimes it especially flips into that because on one screen it looks like the retinal pattern if you shut your eyes—or just cloudy dreams or sunspots.

SB   I think partially there's something about having your eyes closed versus having them open that creates this other space. If you lie in bed at night and close your eyes, you can see abstract patterns of color and have an out of body spatial relation to the room because you're not seeing yourself

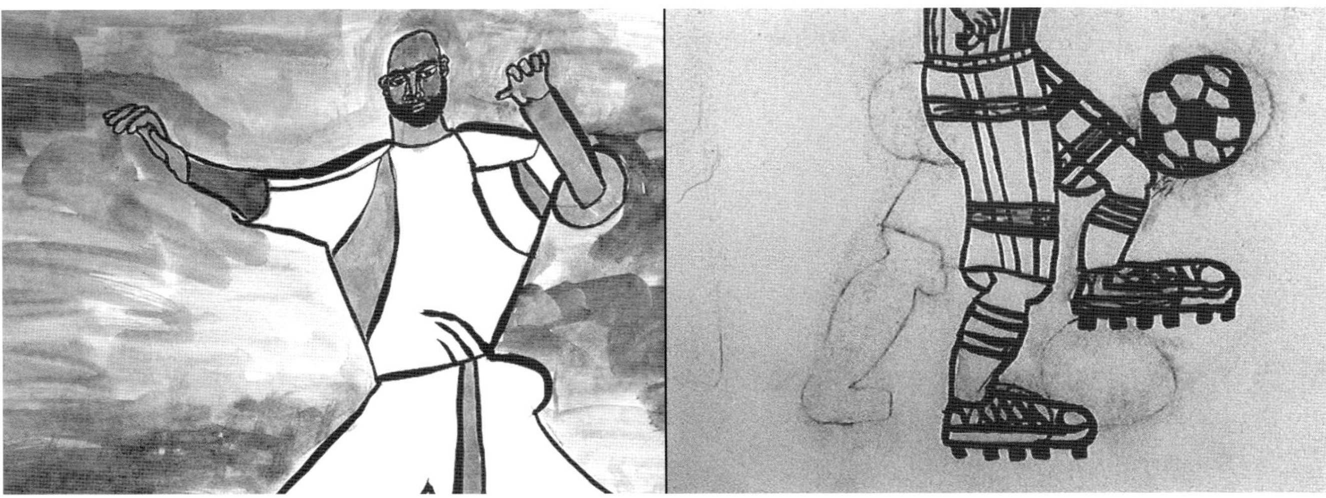

in perspective to anything. You're just in this patterned abyss, and it's only through sound that you understand your size.

AS But I think that's interesting because that's the borderline experience between conscious and unconscious. In classical perspective, the draftsman has rendered the comparable scale relations between objects. But in this work, you have not calibrated those relationships, so scale becomes exhilarating in the same way that gender change becomes exhilarating. It confuses the viewer a little bit to confront this monumental image that questions what's inside and what's outside, what's subjective and what's objective, and what's clearly different between us and the art object. The sense of dislocation is even more extreme because the video is so resolutely located. We're in the store, we're at the mall, we go to the bar, we're at the airport, we're on the airplane, and yet we still don't know where we are because none of the scale relations have been actually mapped out for the viewer.

SB There's something really musical about shifts in perspective and scale, the way music can suddenly erupt into something but then become totally silent. I think a lot of what I do is influenced by listening to music. When I was in the band Le Tigre, prior to starting *Play Pause*, I made drawings that were projected from slides during live performances. From that process I could tell that using drawings that illustrated something without plot or dialogue would work. Being in a band also influenced the way I thought about narrative structures. Creating beats and actually making music helped me to think about having two channels and multiple things happening at one time in a way that is different from my single-channel work. I can see now that editing

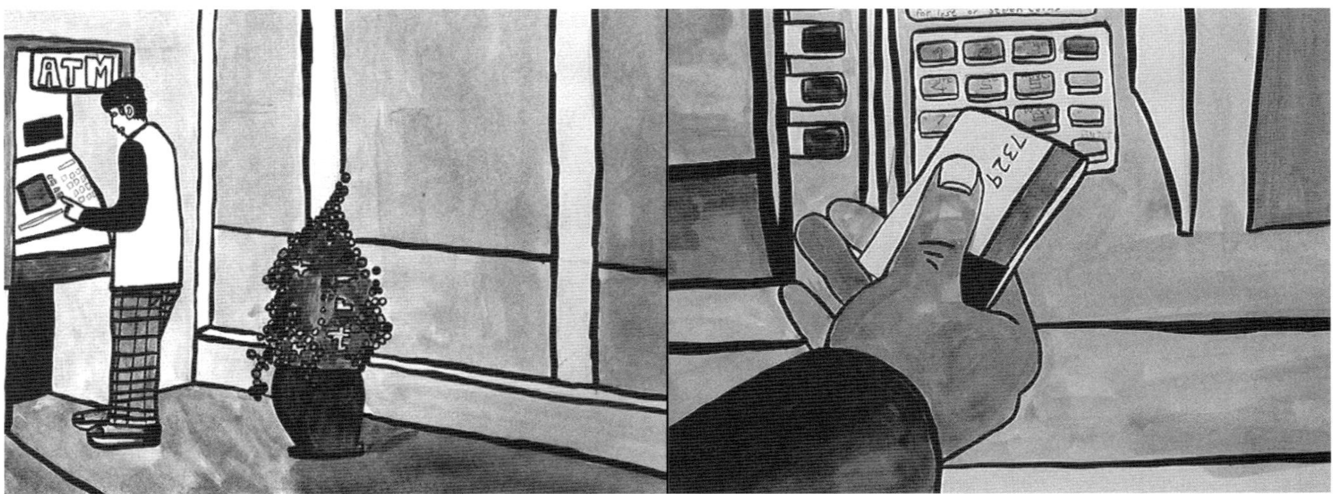

a video based on drawings has a language that is helping me think about painting and going back to music. So all of these things start to form these weird spider webs with each other.

AS   It seems that a zine culture is in there somewhere—like this do-it-yourself world that's involved in a kind of expressive function.

SB   I think the do-it-yourself thing comes from a much earlier place for me. My dad's dad was an architect, but he taught himself. He designed buildings and then sold the blueprints to people who had credentials. My mom is what I consider a folk artist. When I was a kid she created these pop art soft sculptures of objects like garbage cans and record players, and she designed costumes for theater companies. For most of my childhood she worked as a house painter, and then later she became a massage therapist. So I have this really creative family where everyone was always making things, but in their homes or on top of having other jobs. I think my dad was more of a professional artist, and so I saw things that were good about that because he was able to make art full-time. Whereas my mom was probably often seen as the person who massaged you when you had a bad day at work or whatever. There's just a different class structure behind those kinds of roles in the world.

AS   Are you thinking of a drawing video as addressing some of these things? I mean I think it's important that in *Play Pause* there's a complete refusal of a slick method of representation. You can call it outsider, you can call it low-budget, lo-fi, punk, or whatever you want, but it's clear that you're not doing

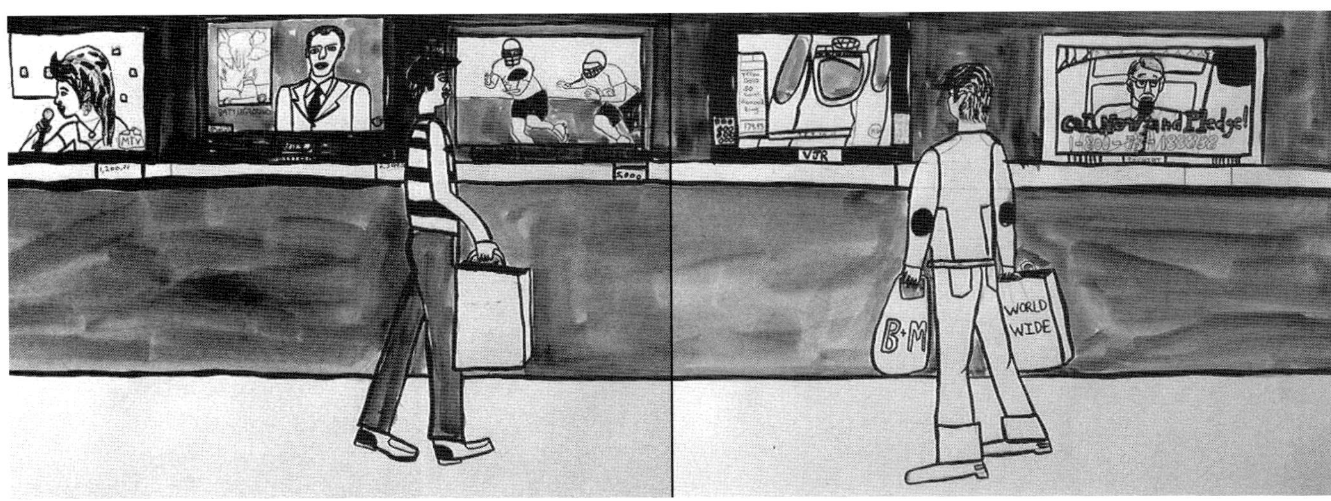

Flash animation (both laugh). And there's obviously a reason for that in this time when all the methods of computer animation and of even the news and stuff are so whipped up into a gleaming frenzy.

SB With still imagery, the audience can project their own experience onto that in a way that they couldn't if the character was all digital and running around and telling them how to feel. *Play Pause* partly comes out of a frustration with how fast and how much talking there is in conventional Hollywood animation. There's a desire to kind of flatten all that out because to me the 3-D stuff is trying to emulate real space in a way that's annoying. The quality of things being handmade is an important aspect of what I make, but also just in terms of balancing out life.

AS The root of what makes people feel modern right now is the ultimate technological speed of things. And *Play Pause* is just not going that fast. Everything's happening at the speed of the way people walk, eat, sleep, read—it's completely orientated toward lived, experiential time systems. I think *Play Pause* is about a phenomenology of being, the way glancing and glimpsing works, detail, repetition, things that are organized in the sensate body…. I wanted to ask you about the head paintings as a body of work. Why aren't they called drawings?

SB I definitely think of the heads more as drawings than paintings. They're bold outlined faces, so they have this cartoon graphics quality to them. However, if you're close up, there's a lot going on underneath before you see the last layer. There's something fragile about the heads even though they're so huge.

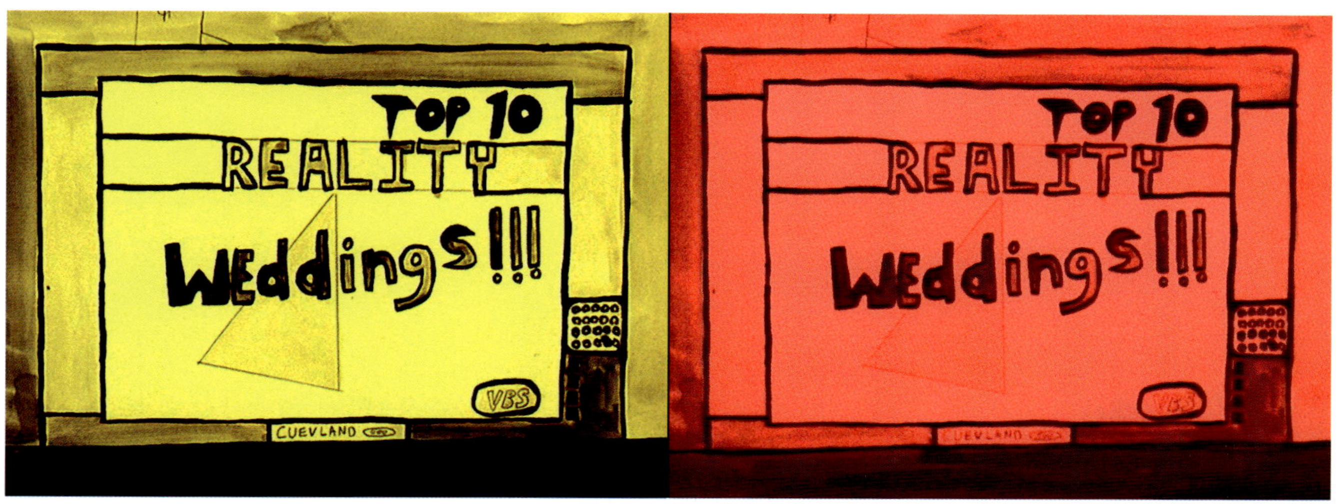

Sometimes because of the chalkiness, it looks like you could just blow on them and the paint would scatter. With the heads specifically I've tended to paint the background out a solid color, so the color is a little bit simplified. The skin and hair is where the detail is, whereas the clothing and background is painted in a rougher, less-layered way—almost as if with a crayon.

AS   In a sense it's a very sculptural way to build a painting.

SB   Yeah, it's more like cutting things out—

AS   Cutting and pasting and building.

SB   I've always liked things that are layered where you can see forms and colors from underneath. You have this sense that somebody spent all of this time moving things around in various orders and then coming up with an end result. It reminds me of Oskar Fischinger's *Motion Painting* animation.

AS   Do you have a studio where all these giant heads can be looking at you and you looking at them simultaneously?

SB   Yeah, they're up on the wall. And I live with them.

AS   Oh, wow.

SB   They look at me when I'm sleeping…. To me some of them have a somewhat godlike relation. They're so big, they feel like they're above you.

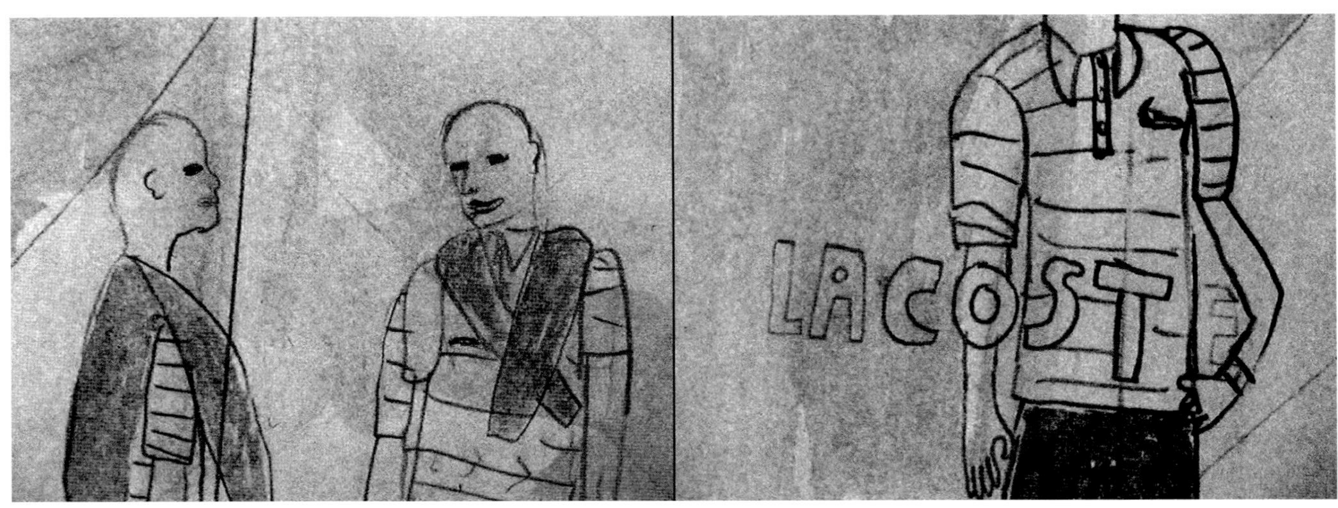

AS   They're kind of like Egyptian or early Roman funerary paintings, but those aren't so big. So there's this strange aspect of the scale becoming other. They're not quite portraits of humans because they're not in our frame.

SB   One thing I was trying to capture in the head paintings is this question of "How does one pose for something?"

AS   There's a lot of that in your early Pixel work, you putting on a wig, an outfit, facial hair, you putting yourself in a posed situation for a camera. It seems like that's been a lifelong habit of yours, to use portraiture fluidly as a costume. Or in *A Place Called Lovely*, you showed people's school pictures, panning across them.

SB   I think I was influenced by Warhol and by seeing Cindy Sherman's *Untitled Film Stills* a few years before I started making videos. There was something liberating to me about the idea of creating your own portraits, or your own representations…. When I started *Play Pause*, I had already made the heads, so I was trying to make something that complicated—

AS   Oh, the video is what they are seeing.

SB   Yeah, I think of them as the witnesses.

AS   I noticed that a lot of the heads are looking down and over even though they're confronting you. A lot of them seem to be looking away a little bit.

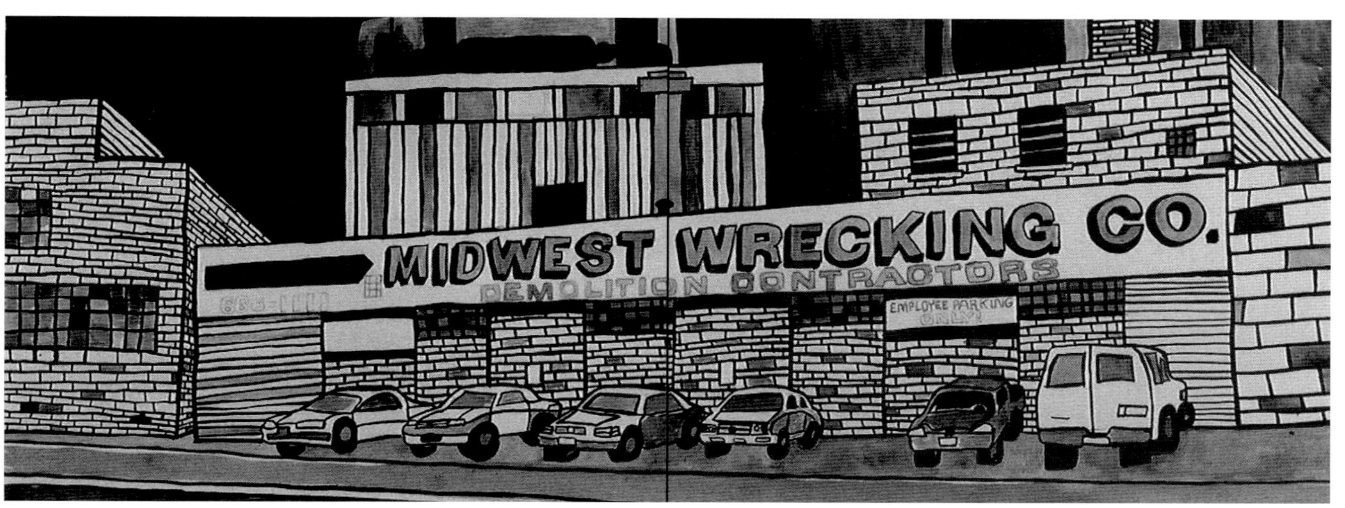

SB Right, they're slightly crooked. I think it's because I imagine them after a while as interacting with each other versus just interacting with the viewer.

AS I'm curious what your painting references are.

SB I'd say initially it was folk artists. And a big part of my painting references come from art that's more anonymous or public such as signage or graffiti and murals. In terms of people that are known as painters, most of my experience with that has been in museums. So it tends to be very male. But I like Alex Katz, Jacob Lawrence's work in particular, and Kazimir Malevich…. There's something about gender and painting where I want to be able to be physical. I think that the heads are big partly because I want to take up a little space.

AS Taking over painting and making painting into something that's not burdened with this very exclusive history seems to be a project for a lot of people I know. It's basically just saying, wait a minute, how can this be a male language, it's just painting, like with a paintbrush. There's nothing inherently male about it, unless you think that the paintbrush is a phallus. But then what's a mop? (both laugh).

SB One thing I was going to say is that with all of this—drawing, painting, video—it's performative. When I'm drawing, I feel like I'm kind of coming up with a running soundtrack of characters and voices and jokes and wisecrack things to say. I'm absorbing all of this language and images from the world

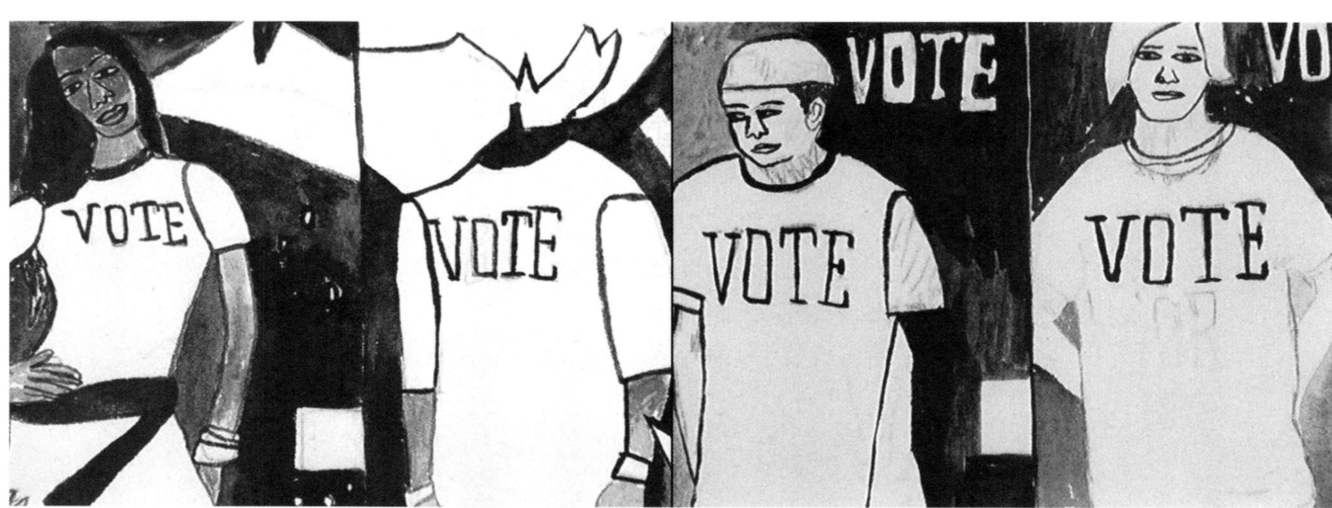

and then acting that out onto a piece of paper. Once the finished piece is on the wall, there are remnants of that.

AS   So that means that the head paintings are similar because they're derived from those voracious moments of drawing as filtering. And I think a lot of your earlier video work plays with a classic postmodern definition of the self as a projection made out of images and fragments from the world. But what about abstract paintings, are they filtering things in the same way? When one paints in one's studio alone, making formal decisions about color and texture—is that performative?

SB   I think there's an improvisational quality to painting where you're making things up as you go along and it's this form that is free to become something. That's what I love about painting and what I think is related to performance. It's the improv of making the space that's not otherwise there.

MAY 2006, NEW YORK CITY
Edited by Solveig Nelson.

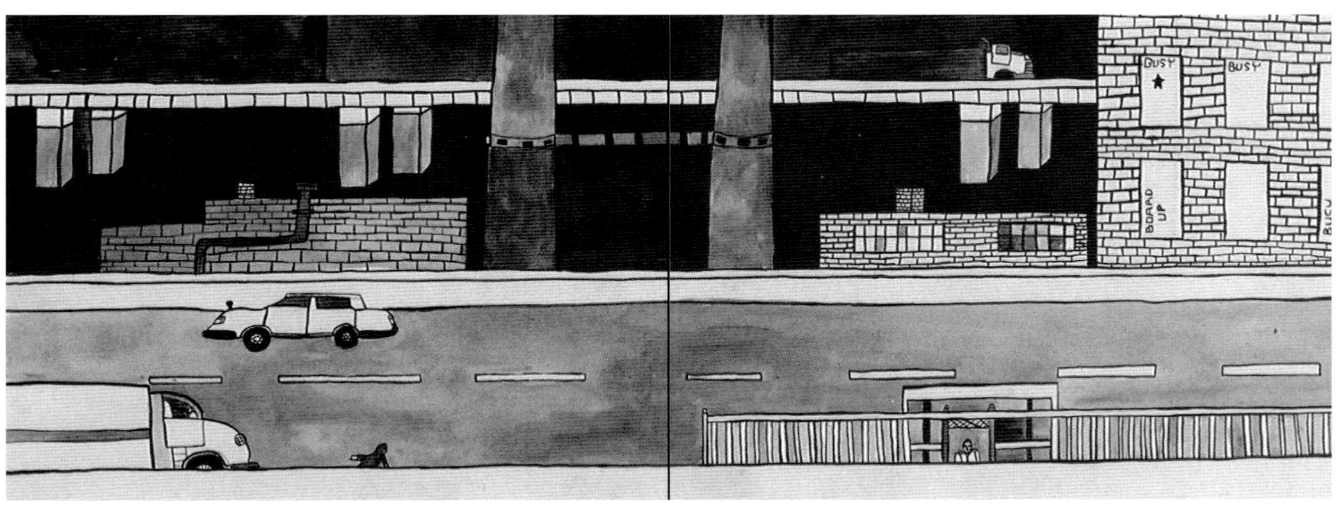

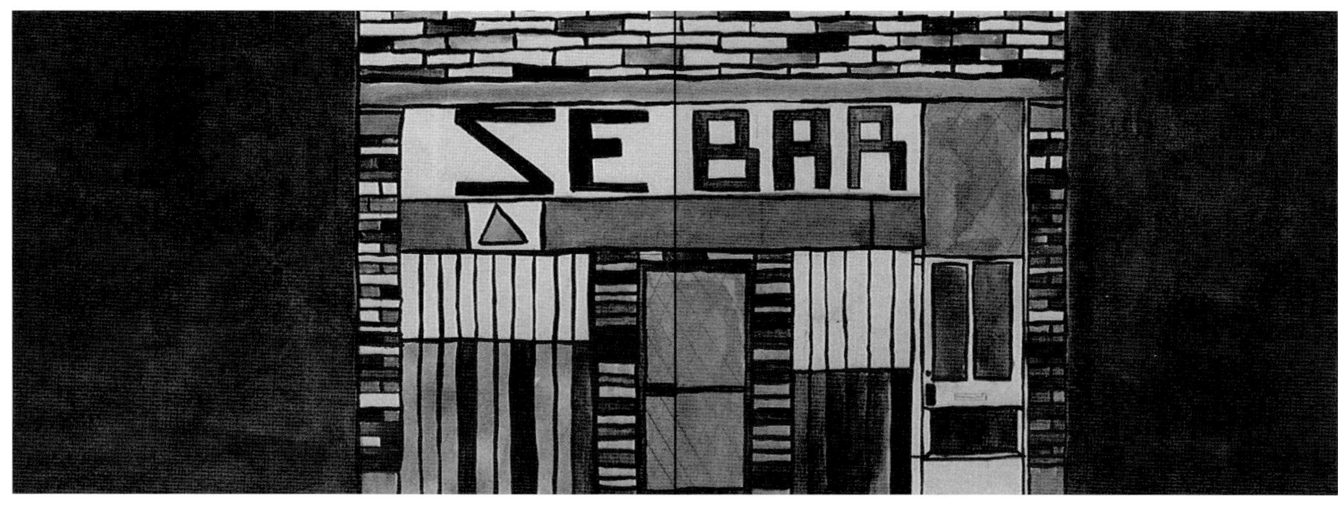
SE BAR

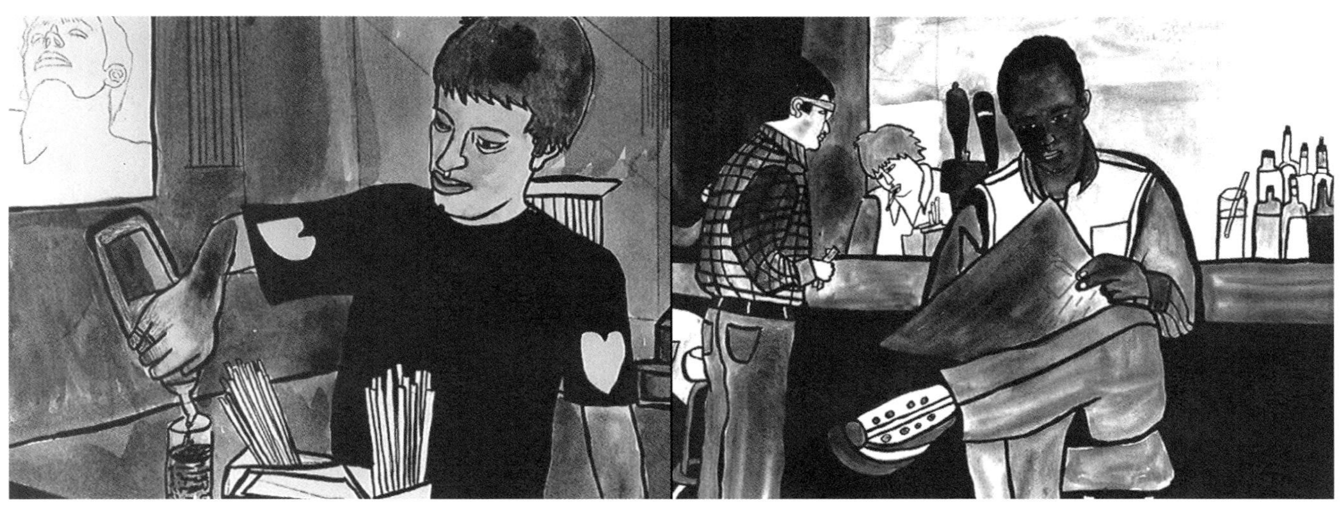

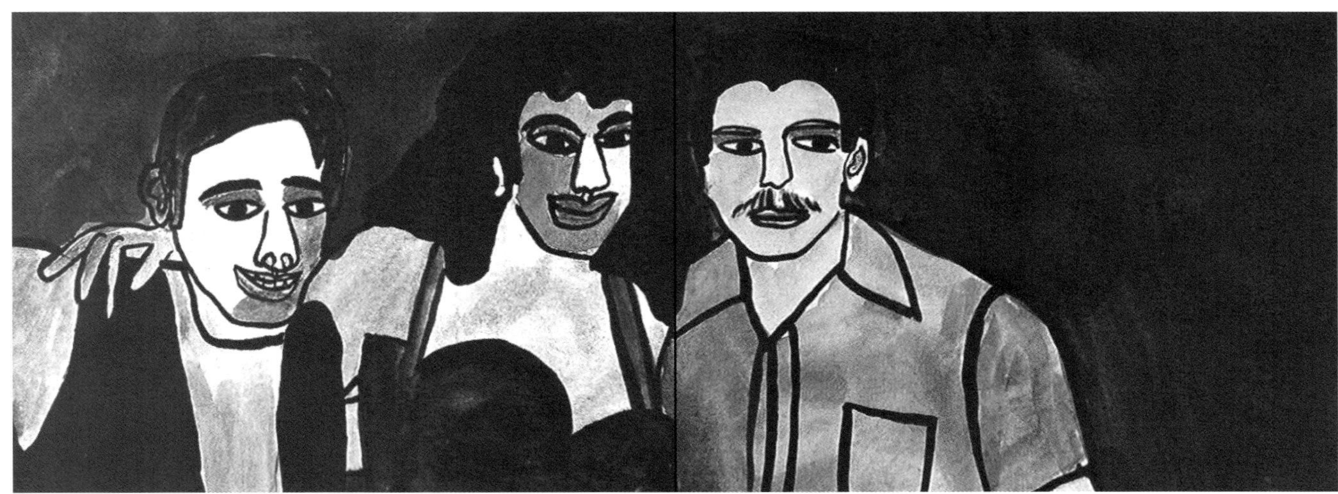

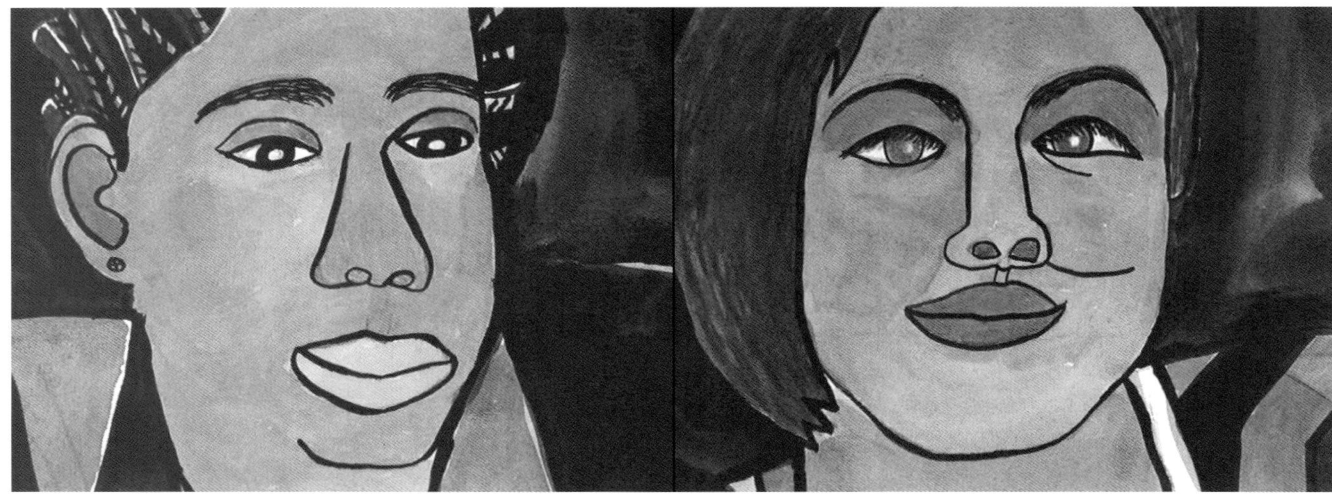

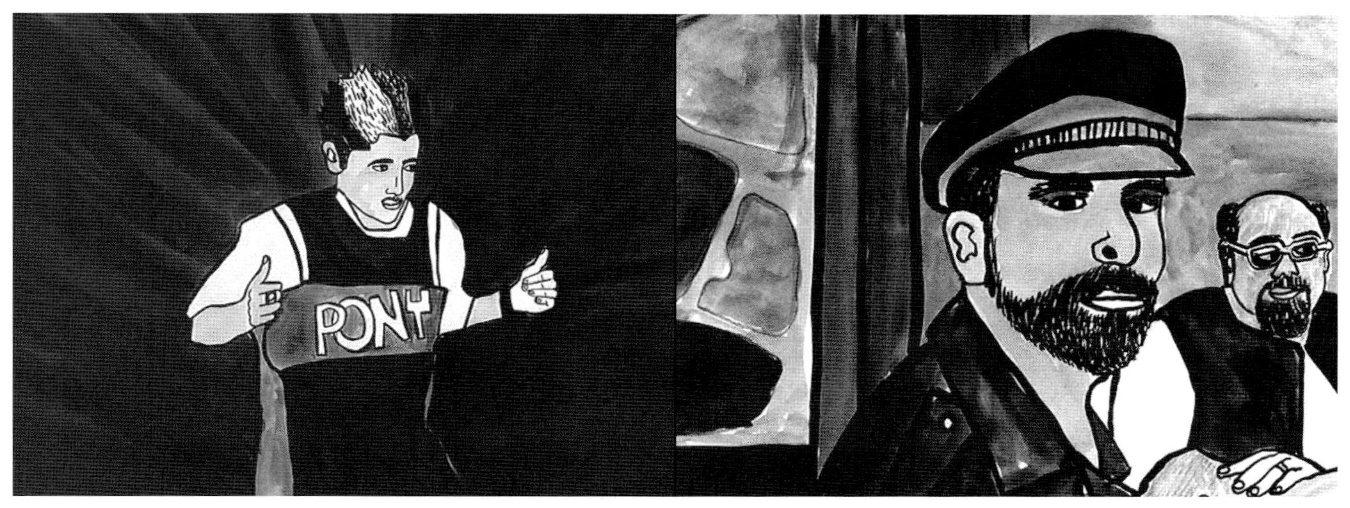
PONY

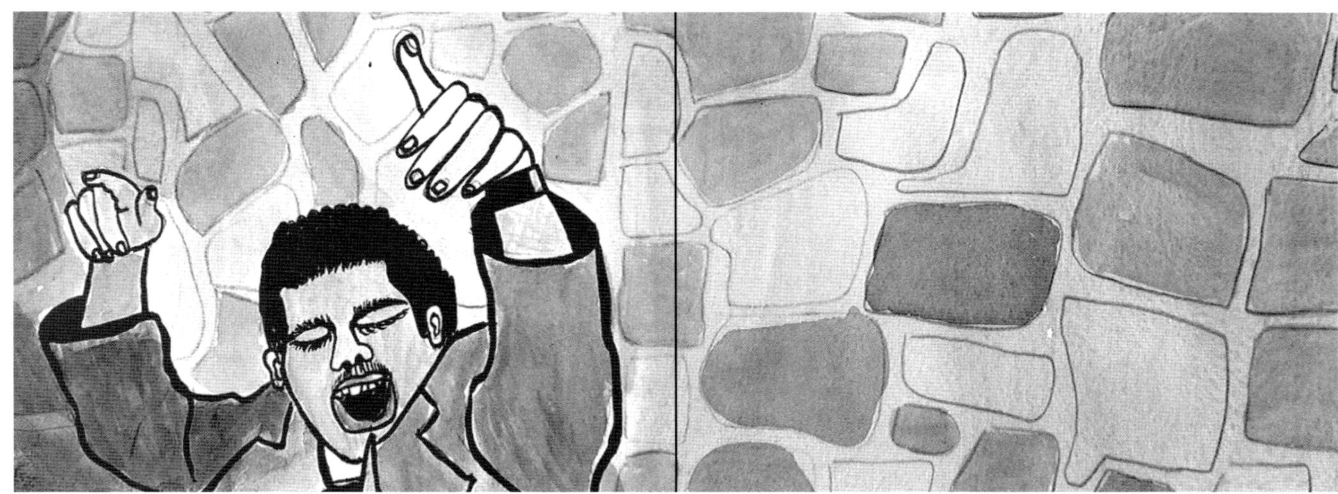

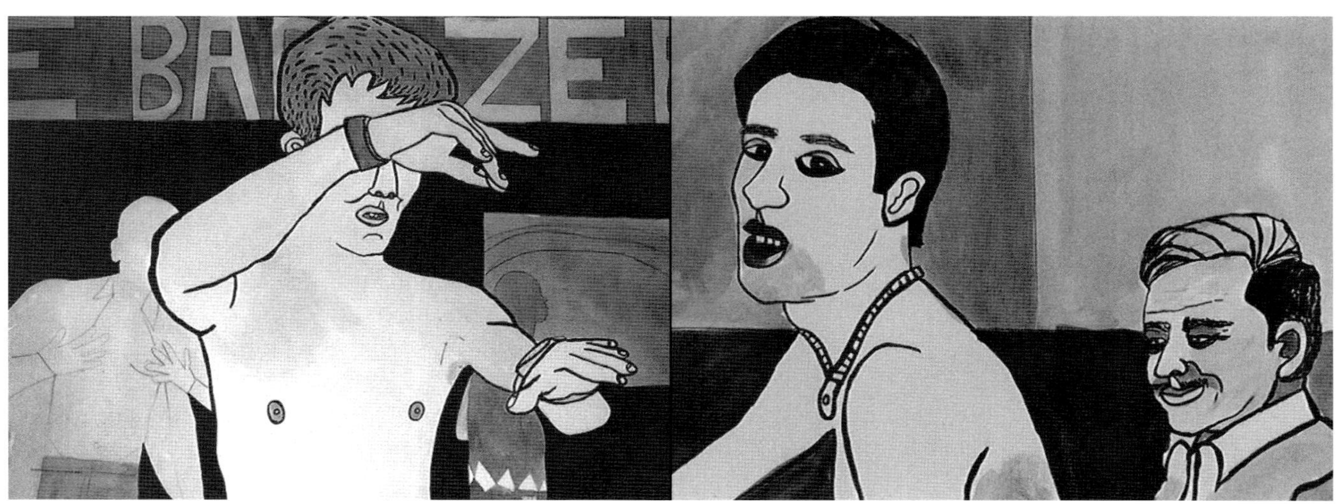
BAR ZE

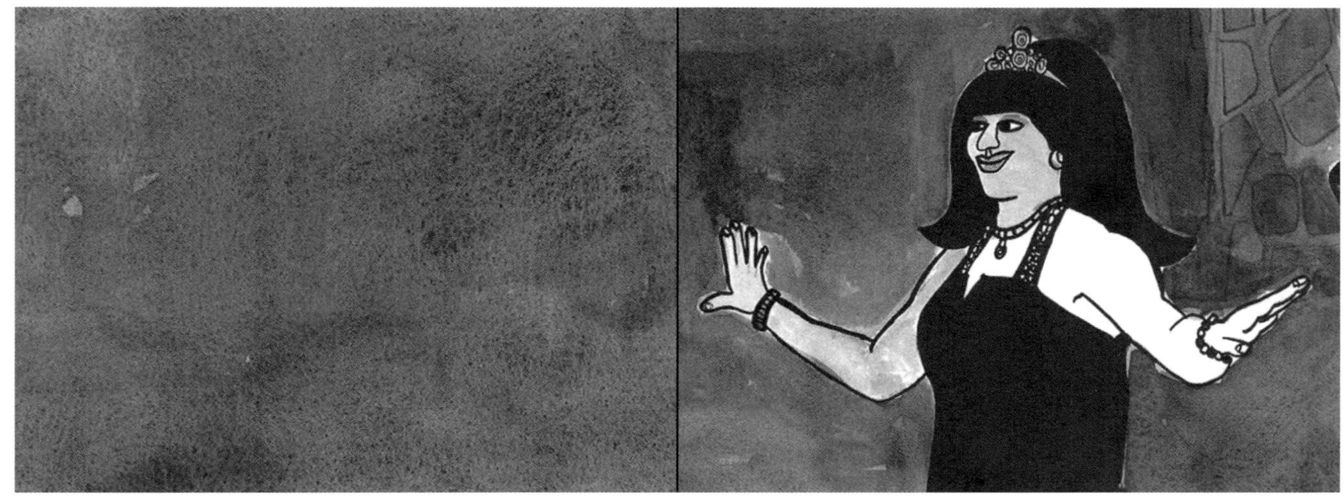

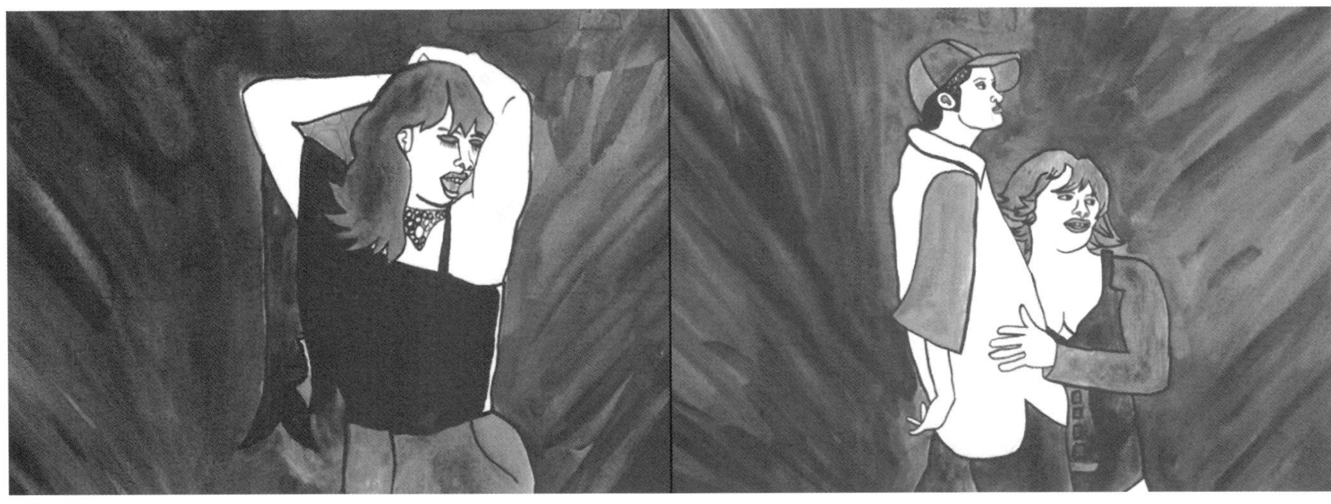

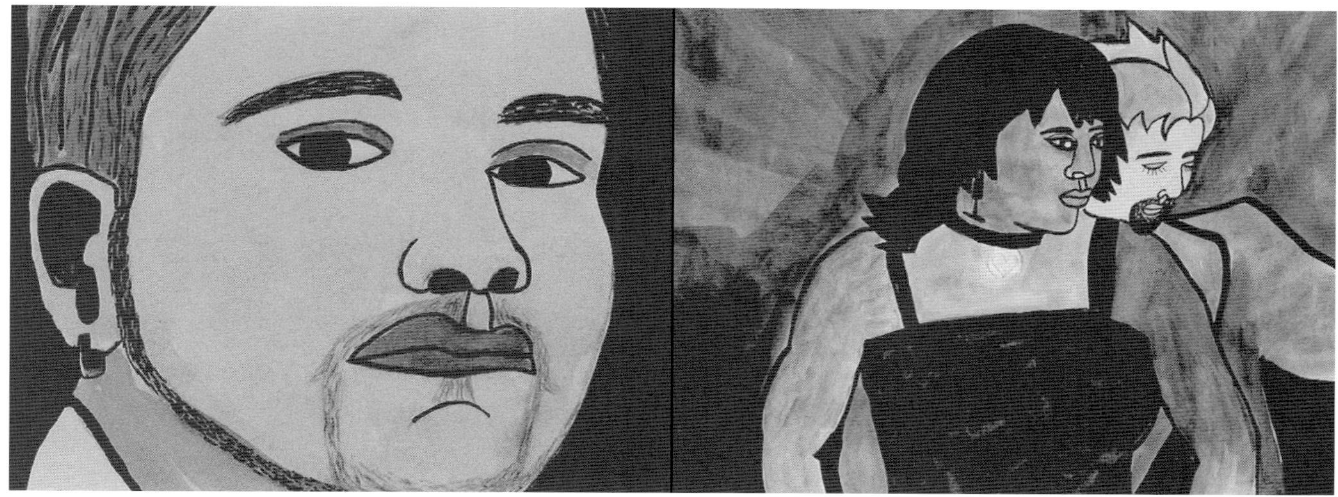

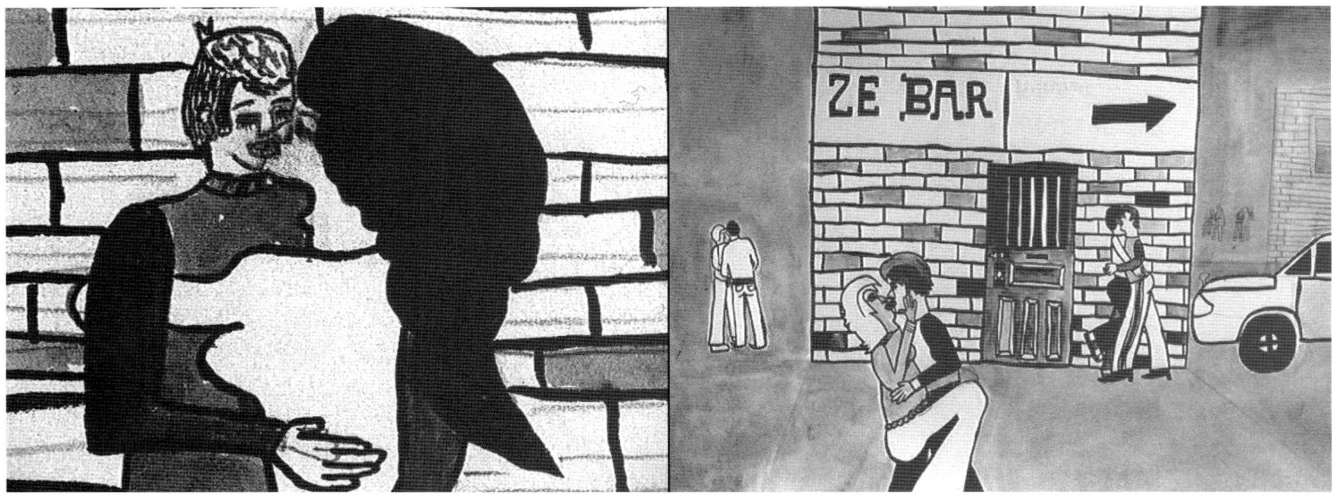
ZE BAR

Paintings

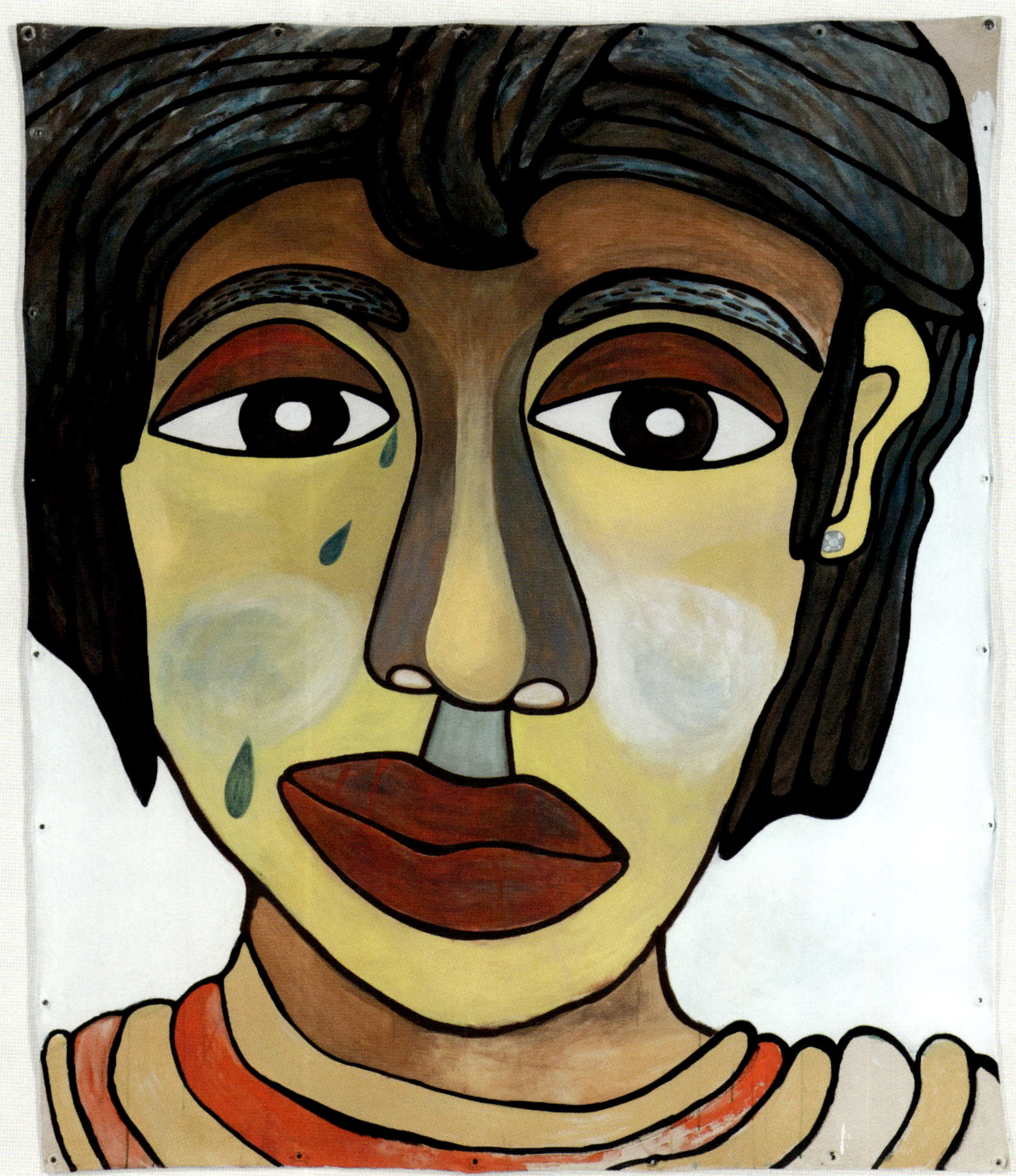

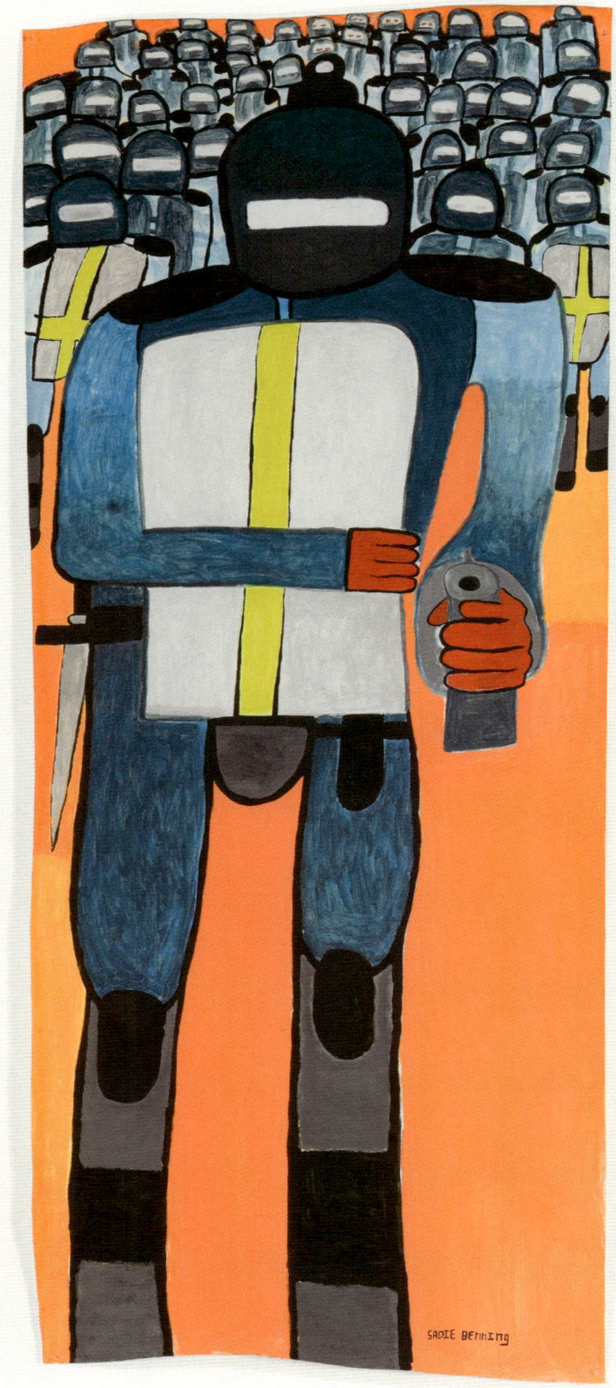

SADIE BENNING

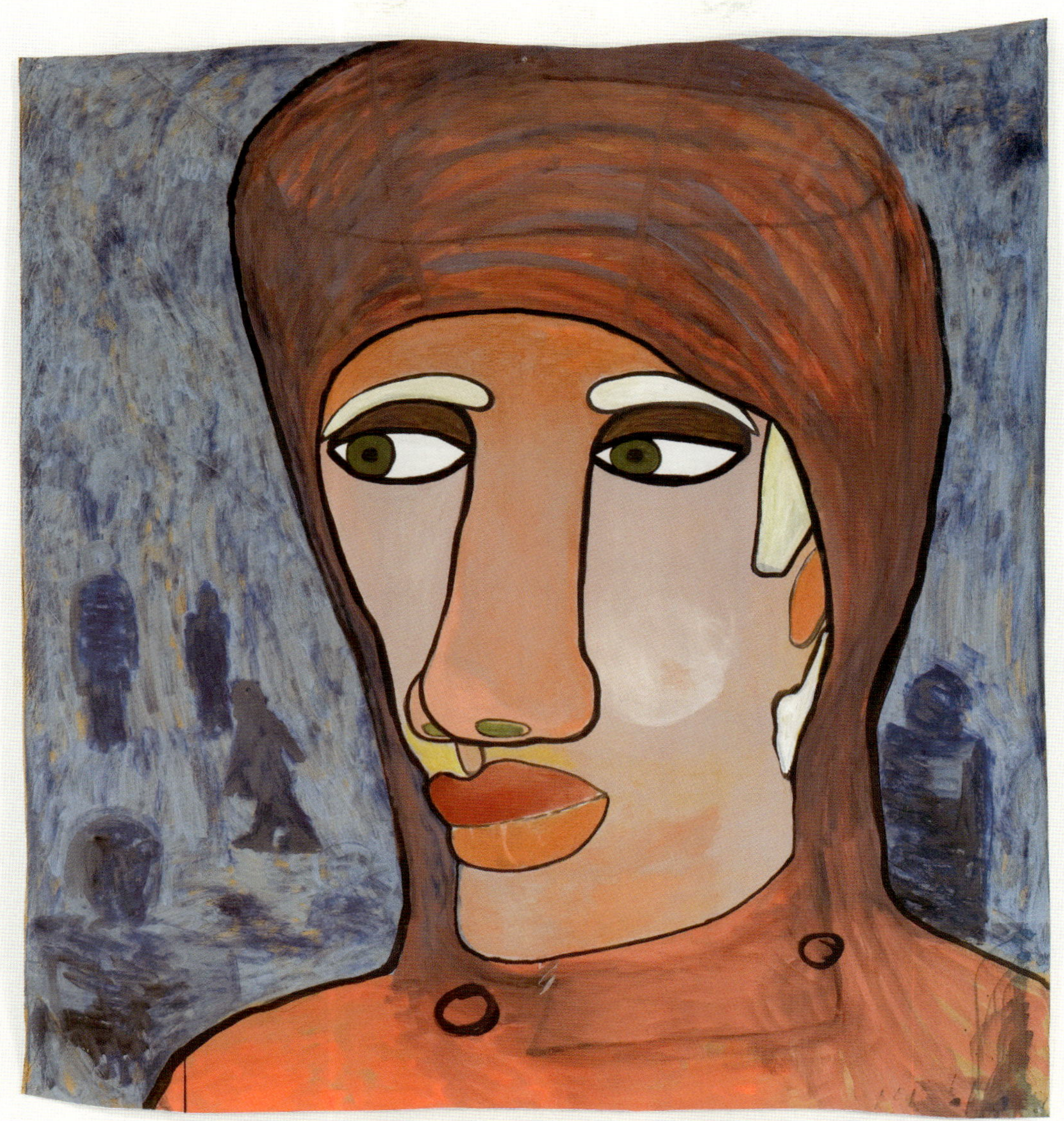

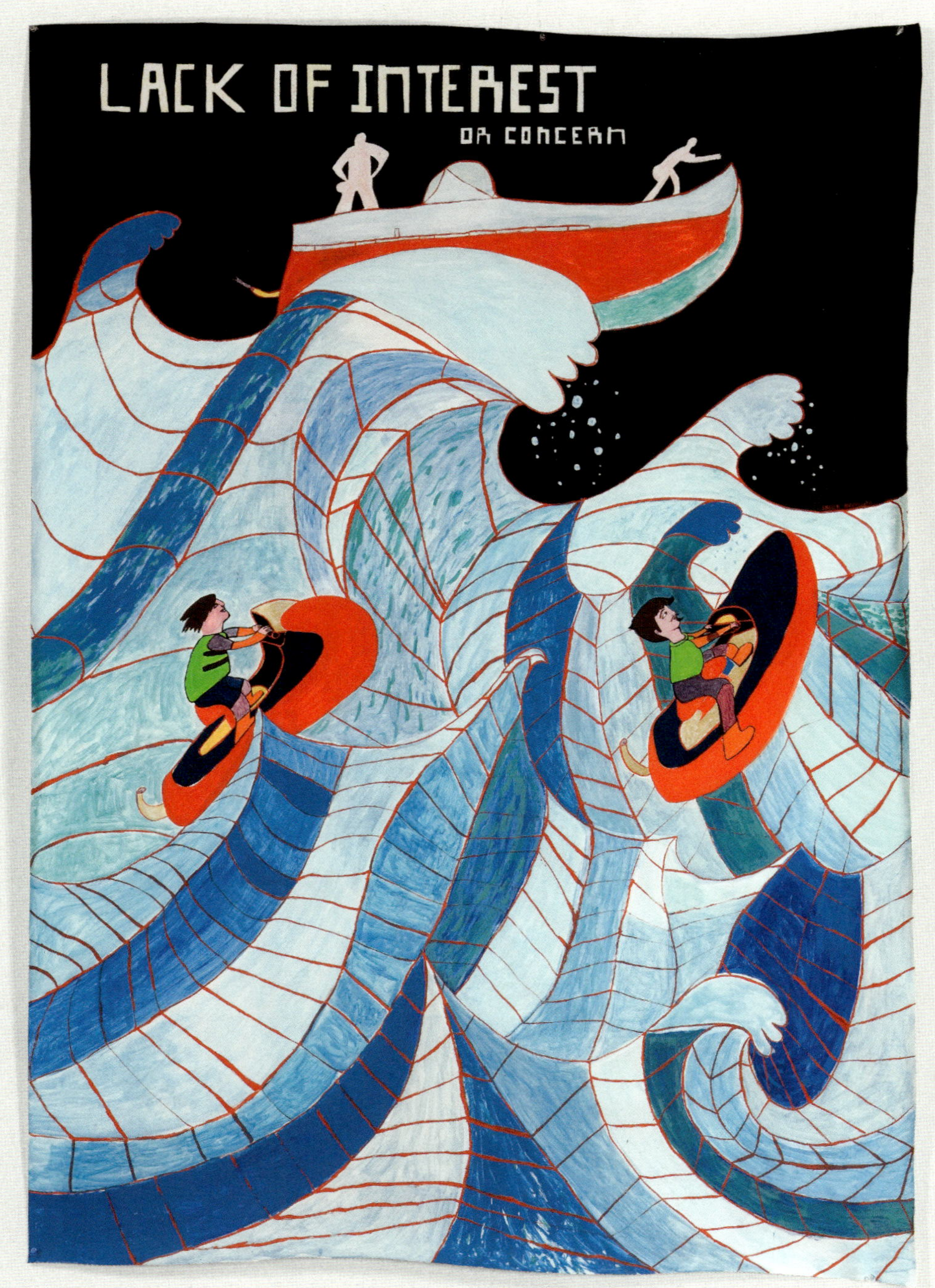
LACK OF INTEREST
OR CONCERN

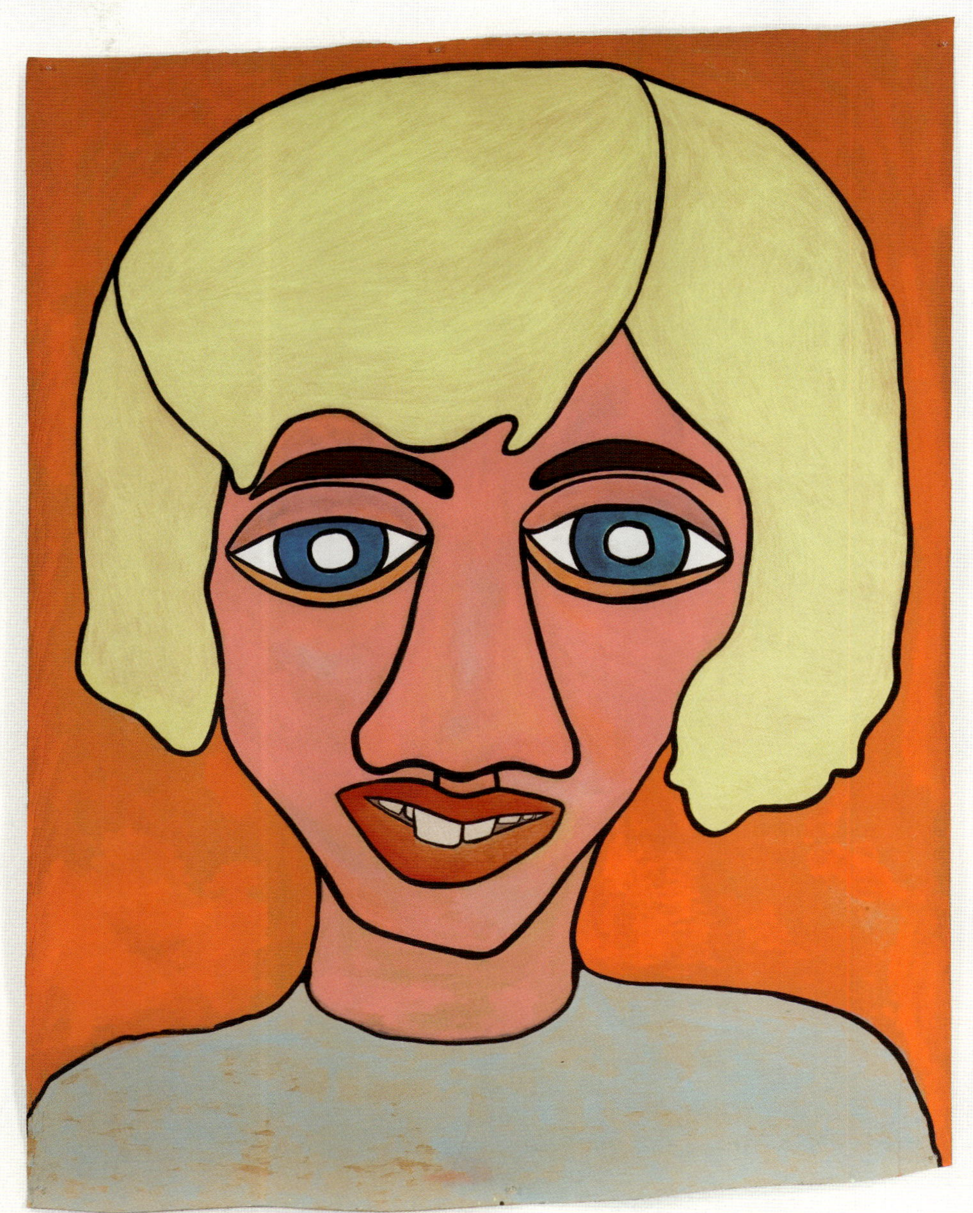

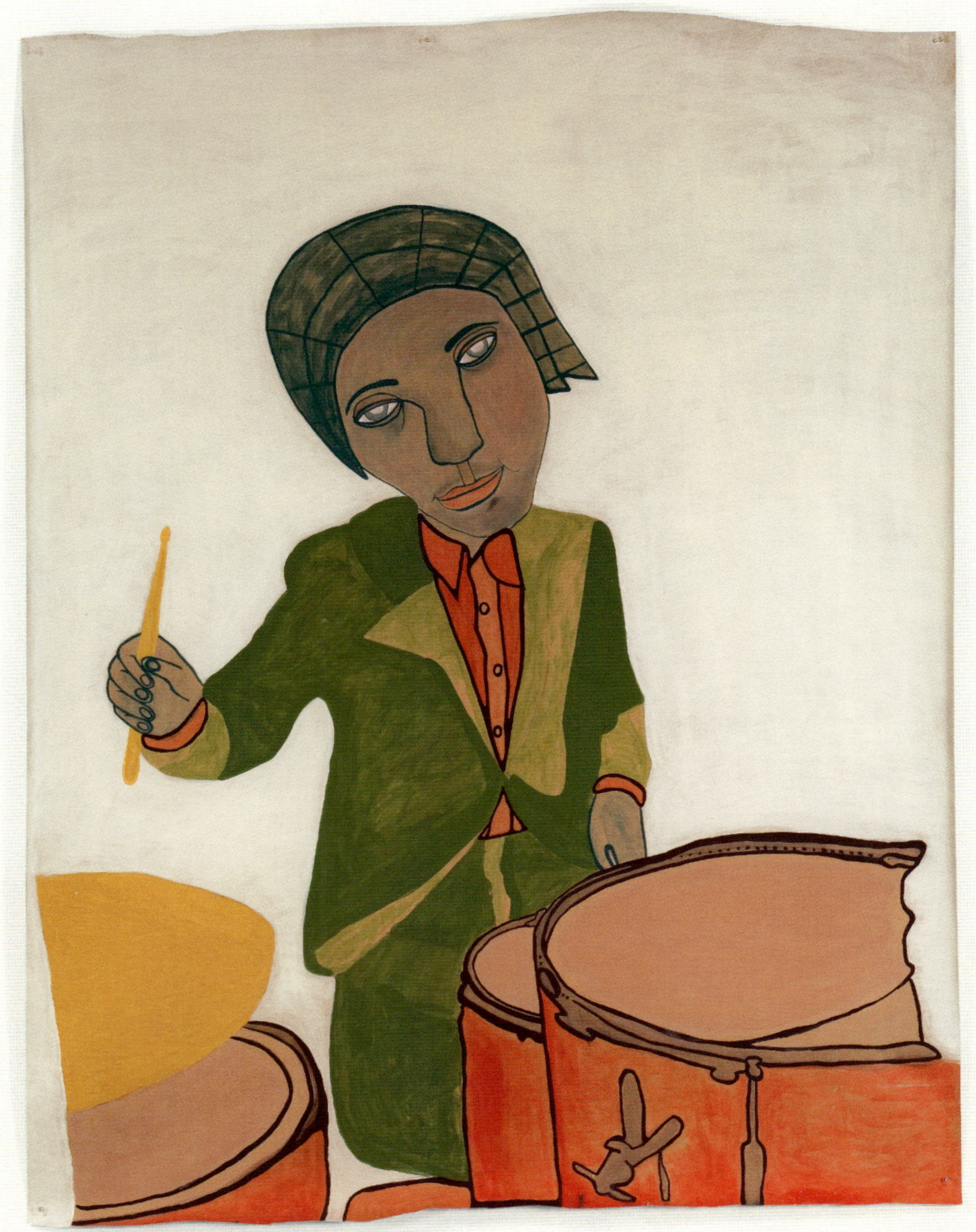

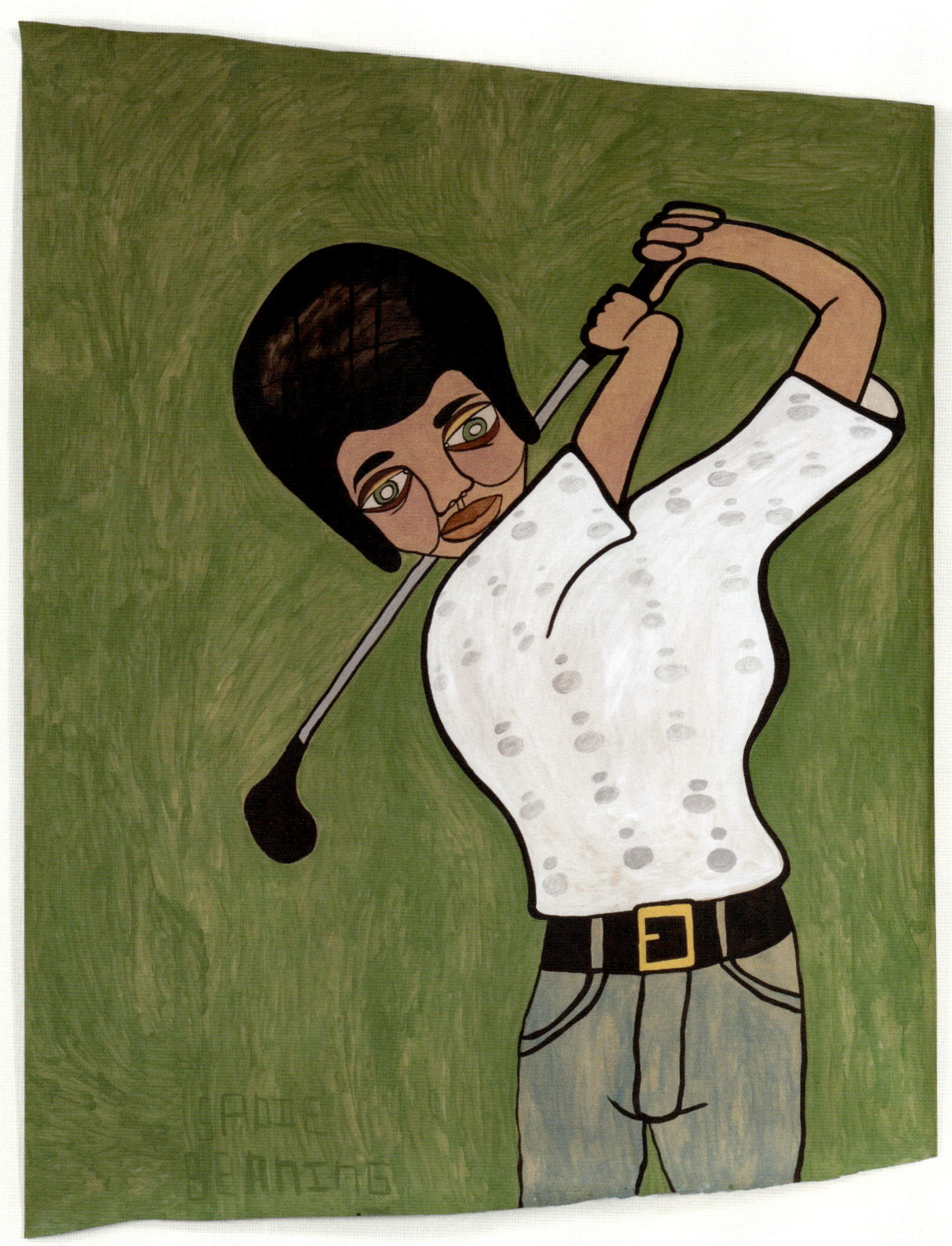
LADDIE
JENNING

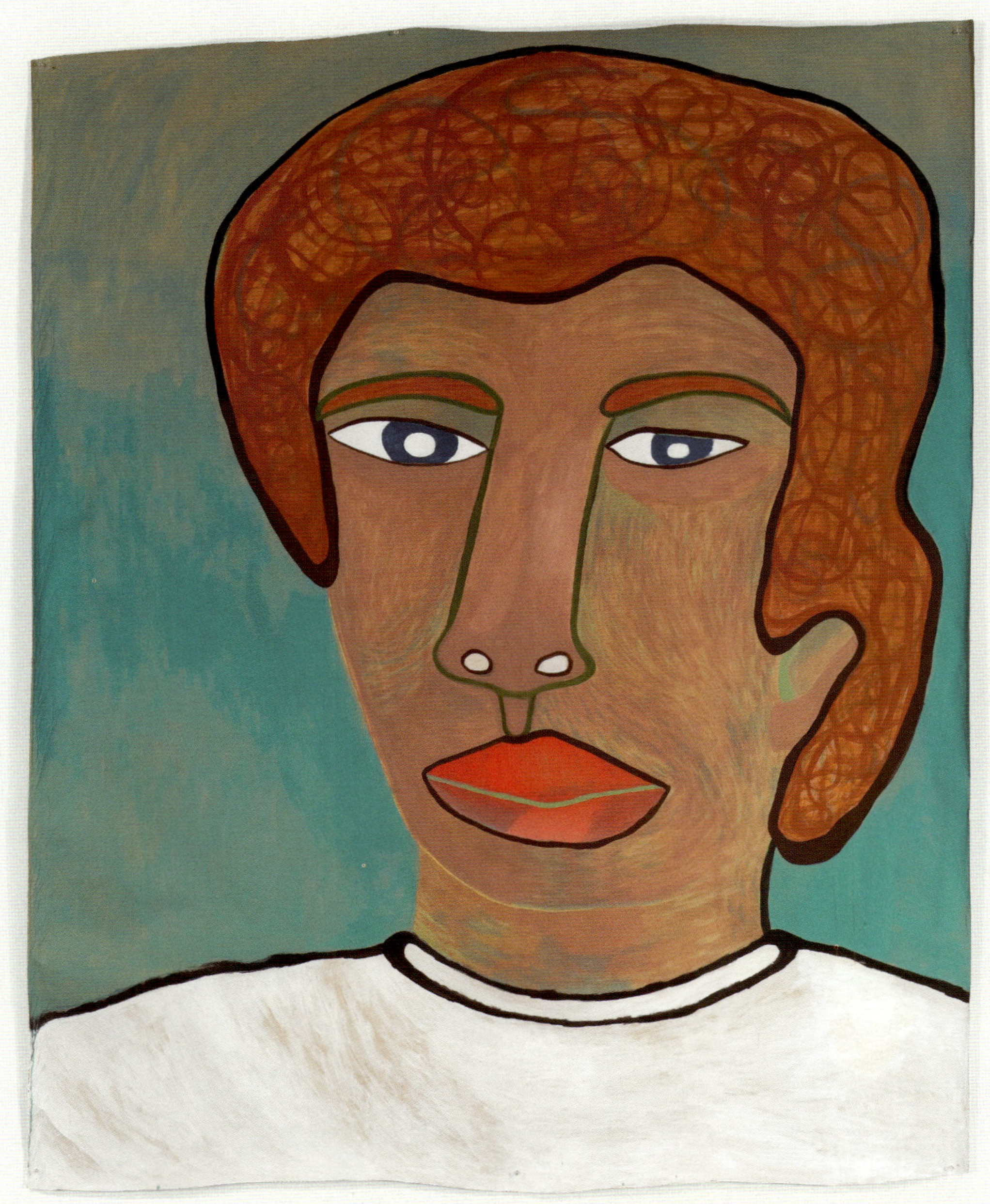

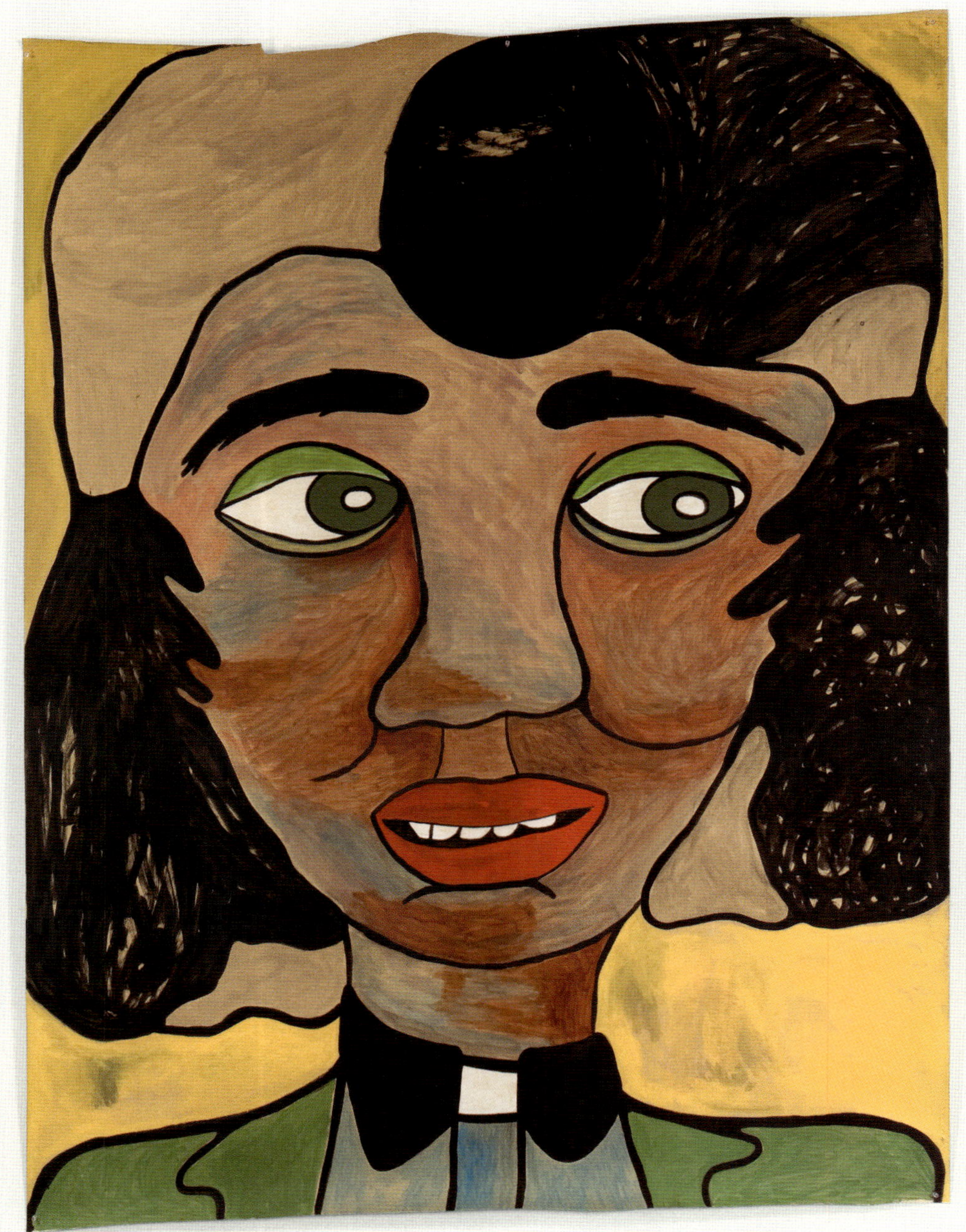

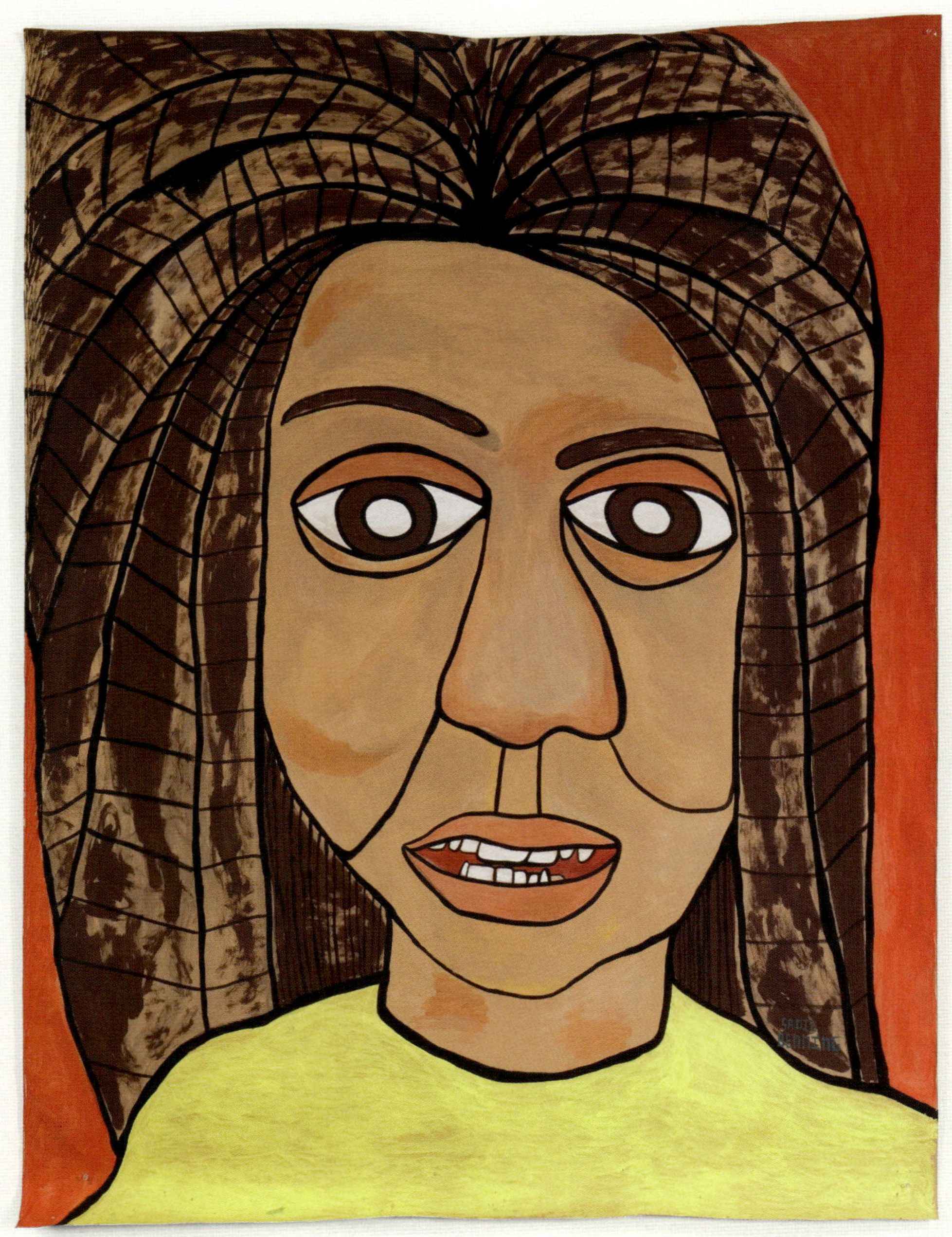

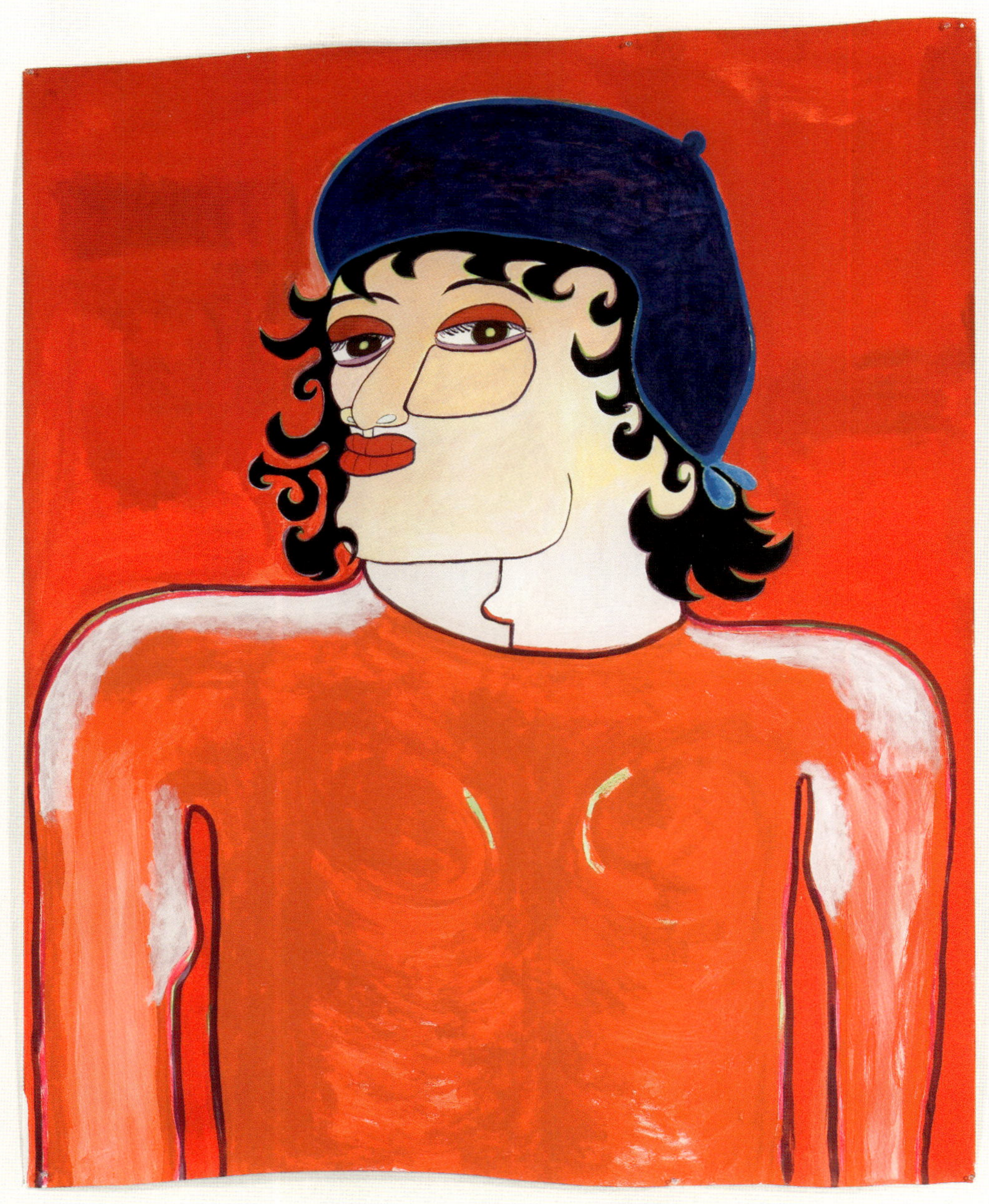

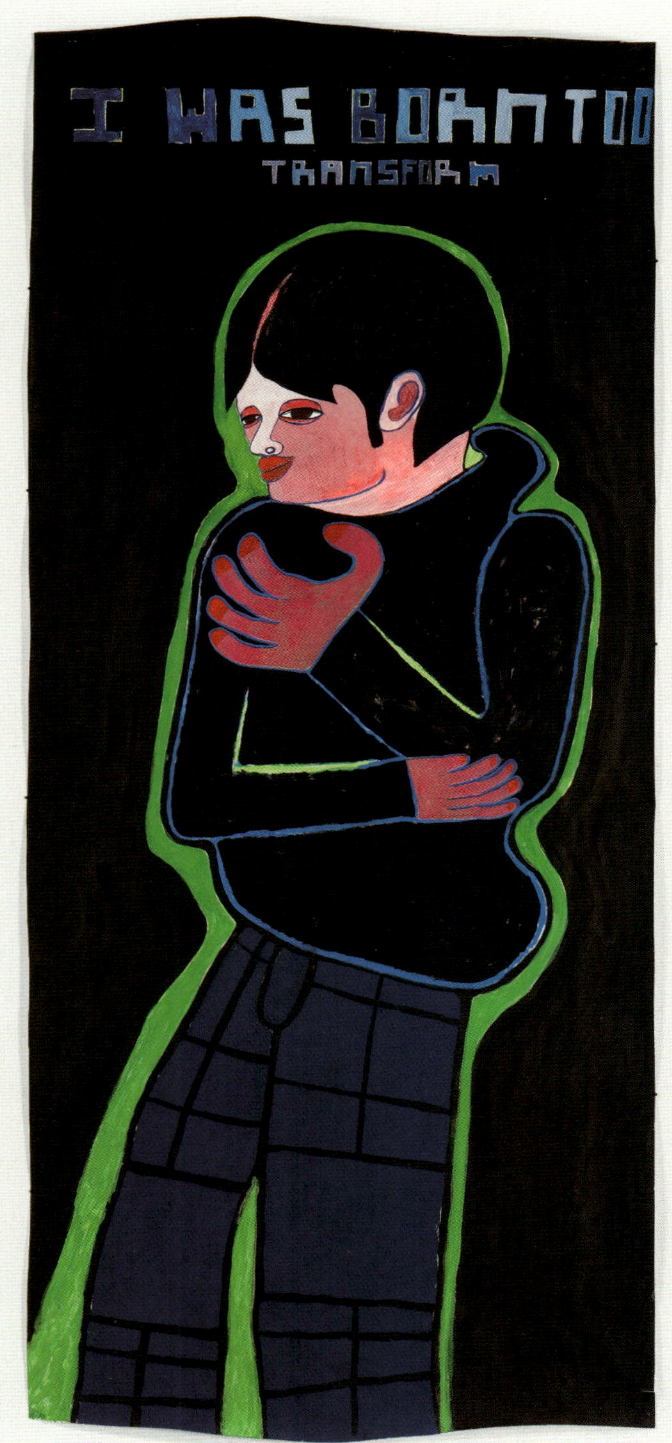
I WAS BORN TOO
TRANSFORM

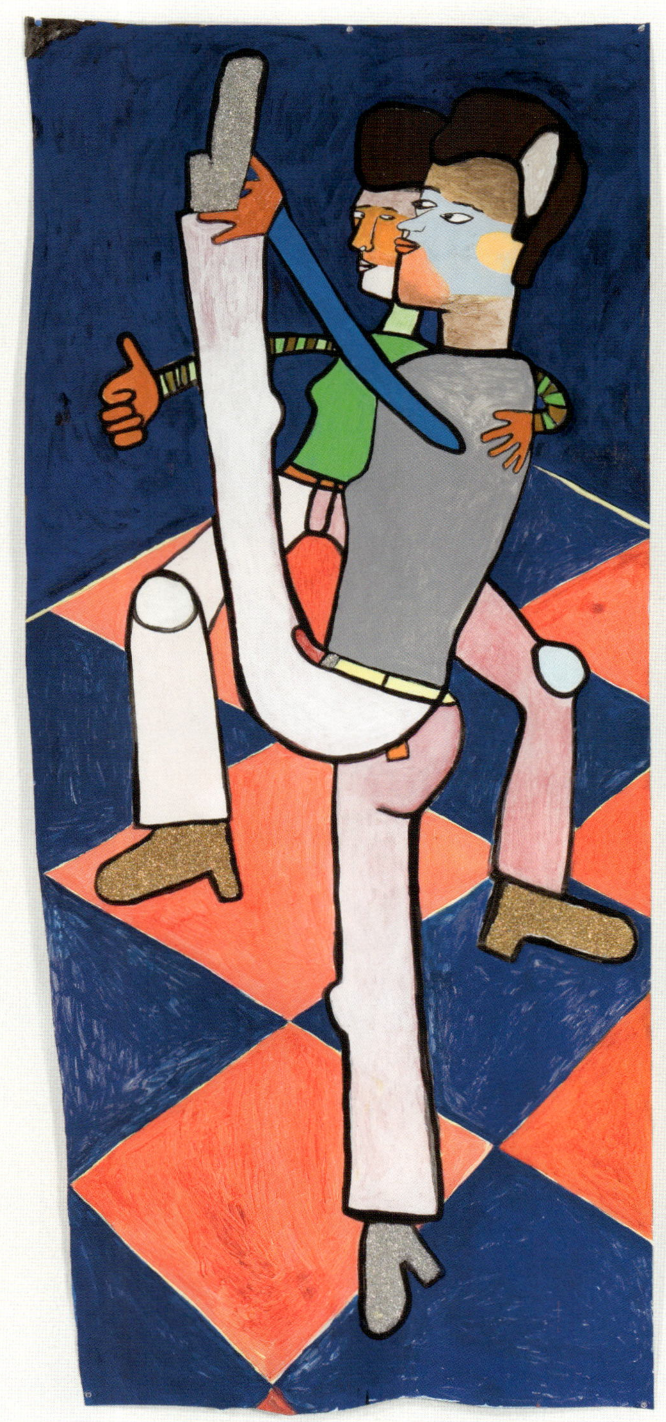

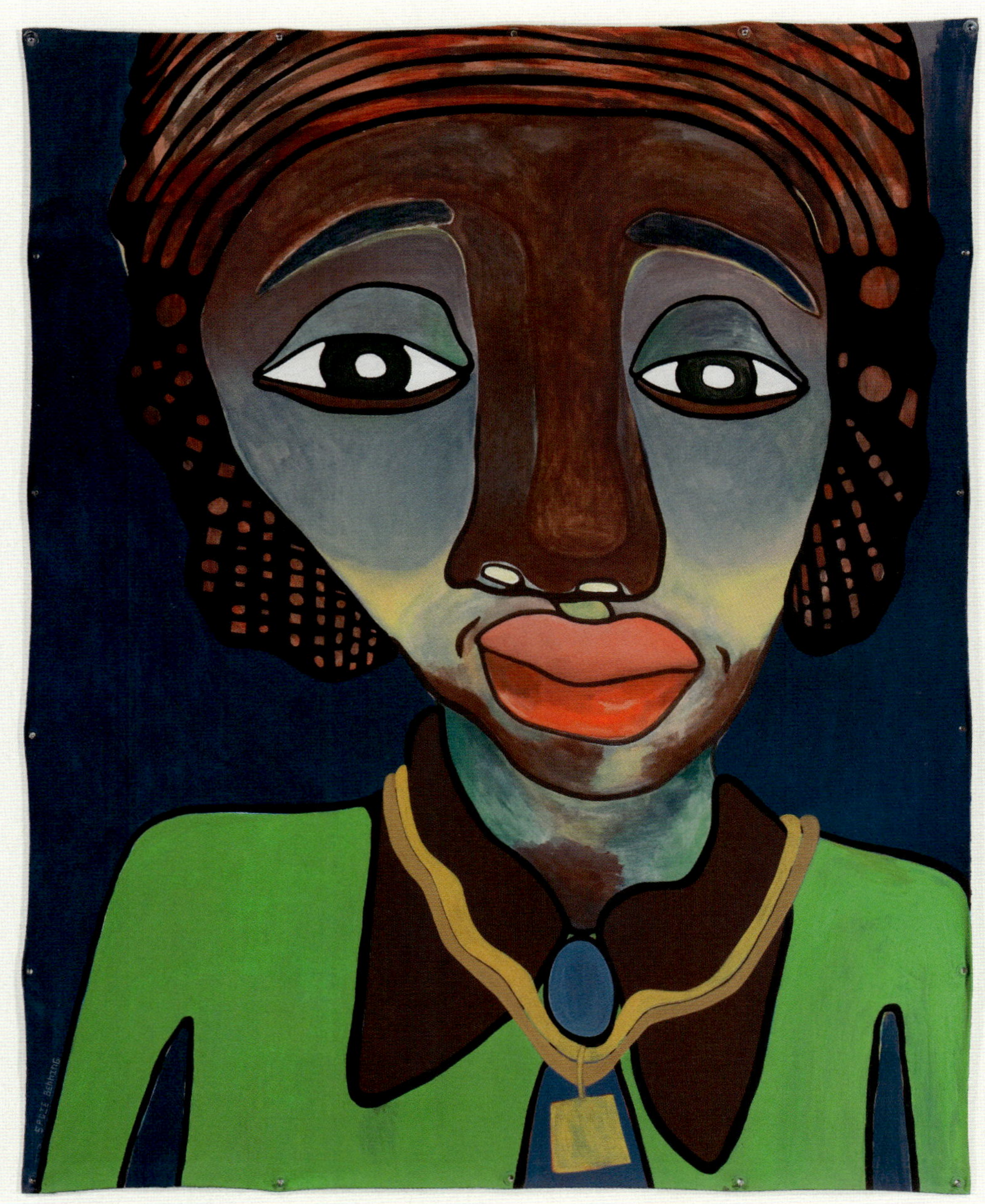

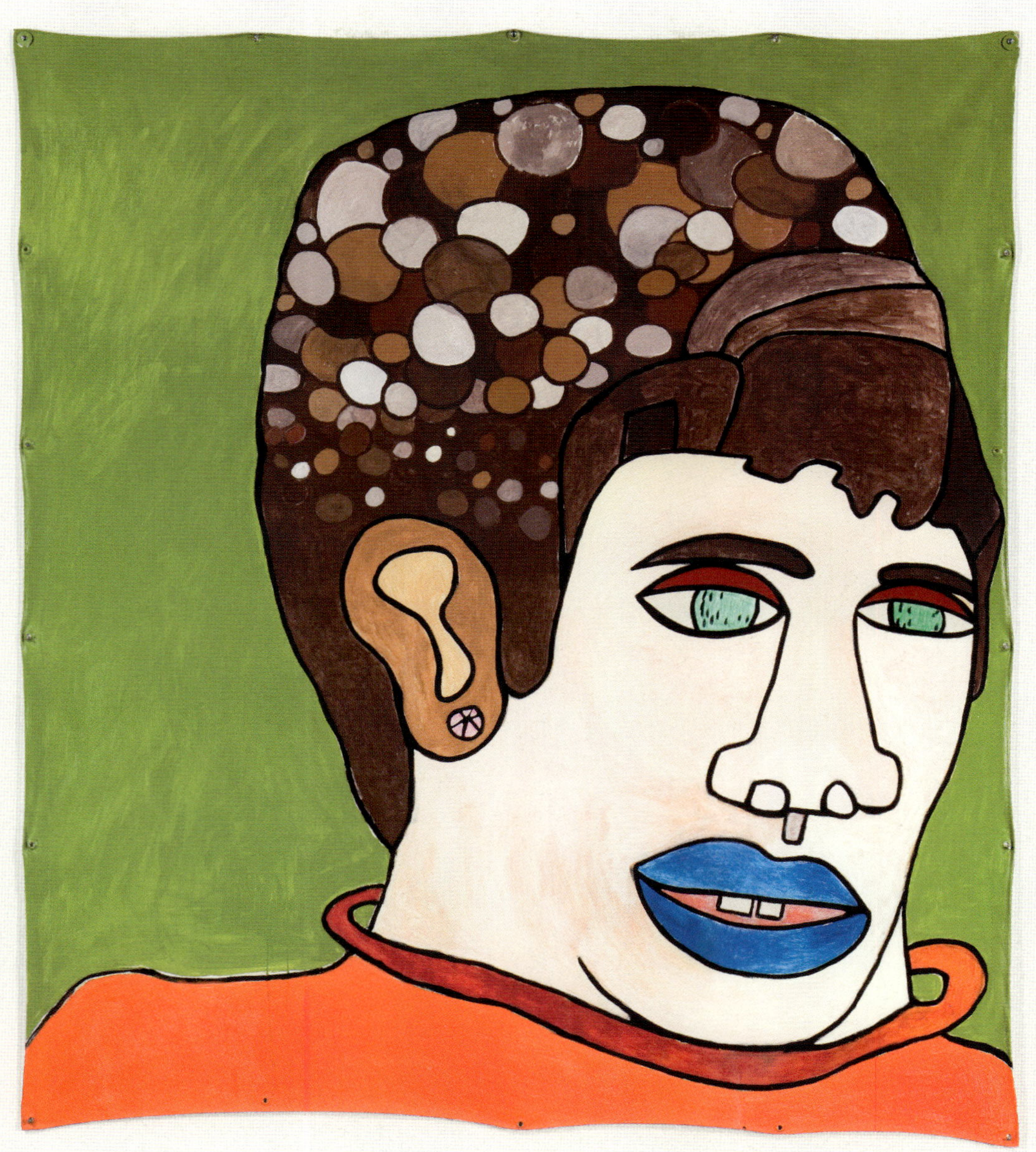

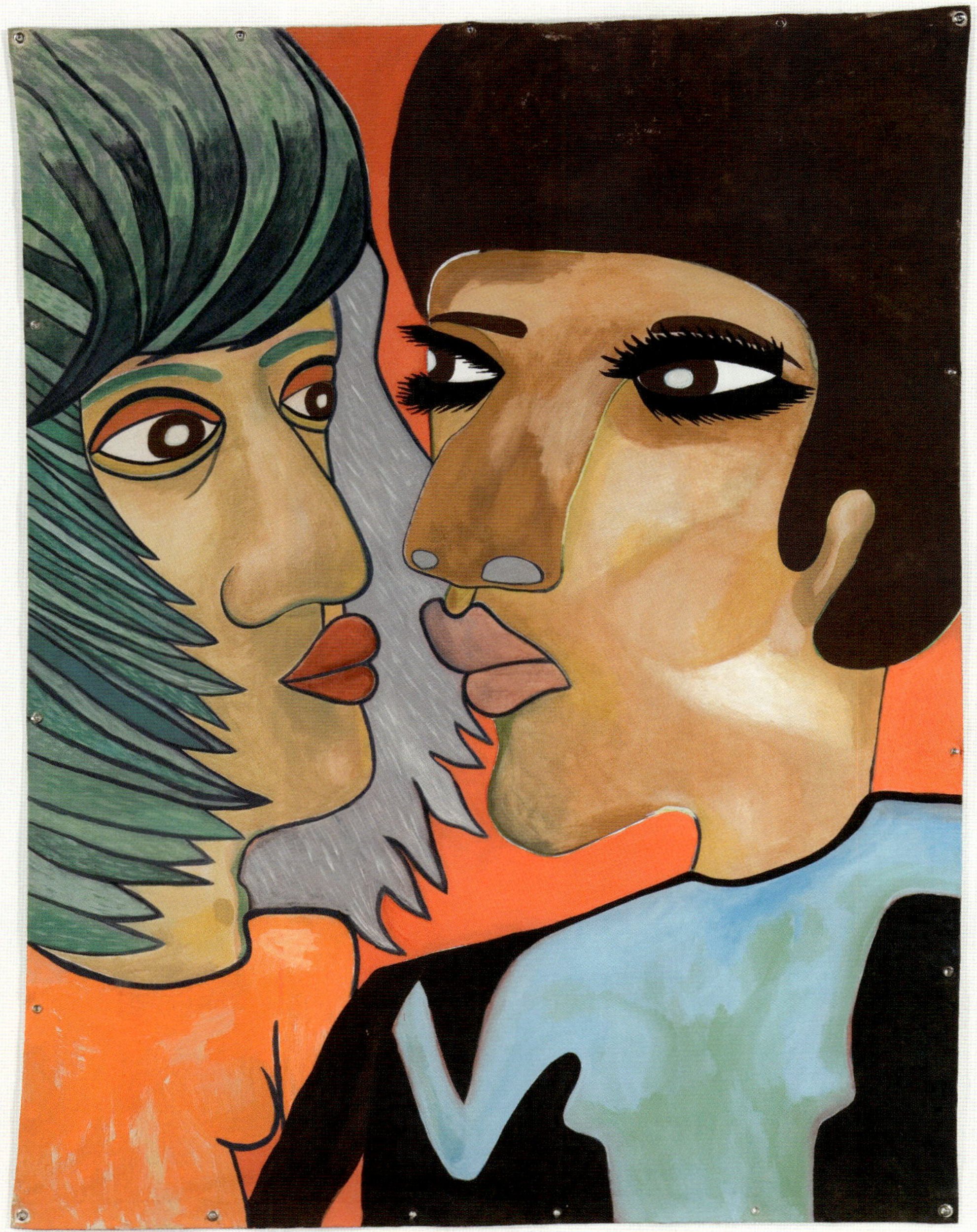

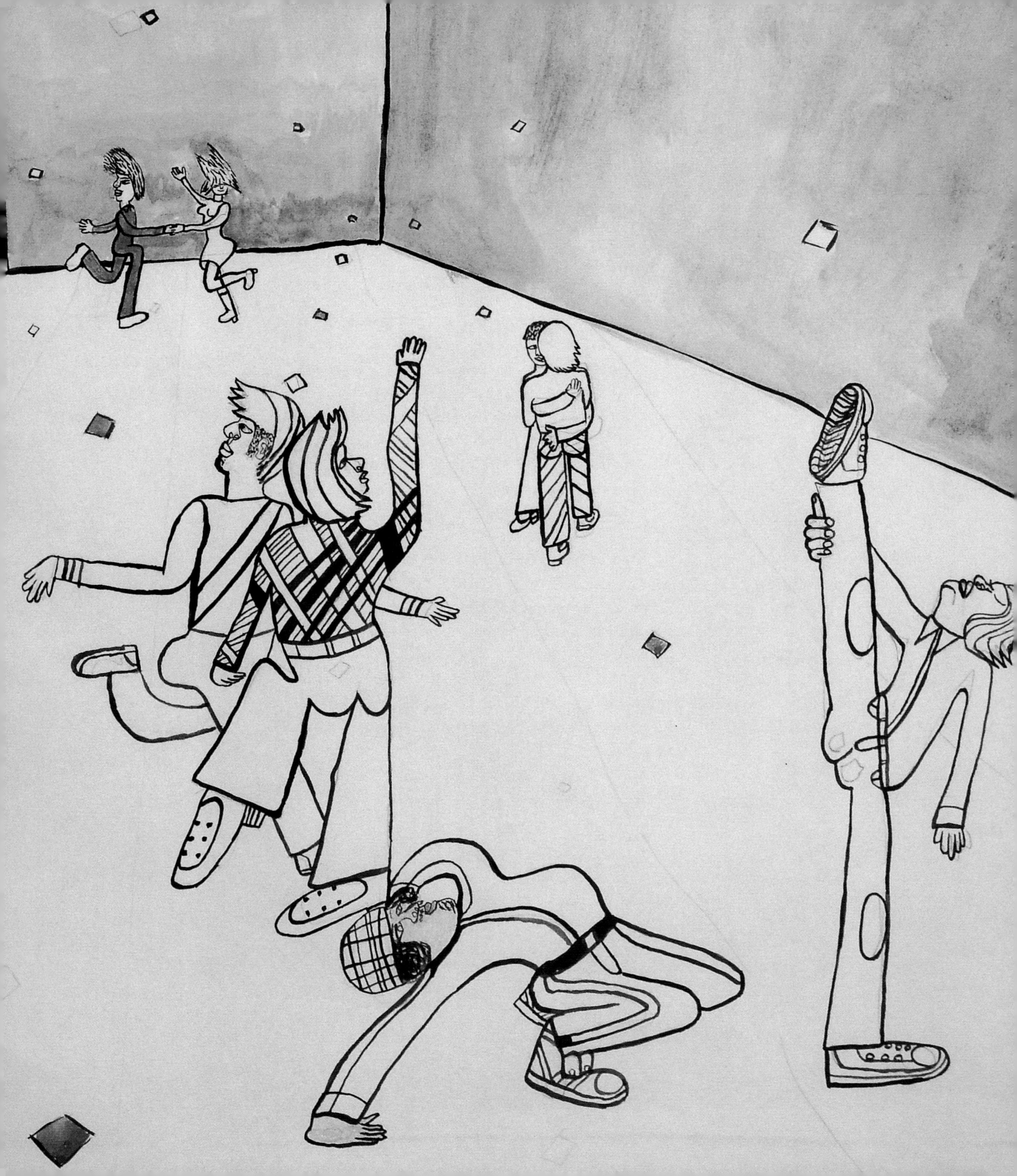

Helen Molesworth

In *Suspended Animation* Sadie Benning offers two startlingly new bodies of work, especially for those familiar only with the videos she made while a teenager with a Pixelvision camera. The exhibition consists of a double-screen still-animation projection, *Play Pause,* and a suite of monumental paintings of faces. The faces are ambiguously gendered, and usually the race or ethnicity of the subject is also unclear. Painted in a palette of bright colors and saturated hues, with a strong graphic line, they are reminiscent of paintings by artists as diverse as German expressionist Emil Nolde (1867–1956) and American painter Beauford Delaney (1901–1979), a leader of the Harlem Renaissance. Aquamarine blues, tomato reds, and verdant greens predominate, pushing the putative neutrality of flesh tones out of the picture. The heads seem to swell in order to meet the edges of the canvas, like animals making themselves appear larger in the face of an enemy. Clocking in at nearly eight feet high the heads do more than simply return the gaze of the viewer; they confound it. Somewhere between ancient Olmec statues and the comic balloons of the Macy's Thanksgiving Day Parade, the heads feel like they are both rock solid and somehow freed of the limitations set by gravity.

Although the paintings share the format of institutionalized pictures—mug shots, driver's licenses, yearbook photos, work ID badges, complete with their weird icy blue backgrounds—the awkward warmness of the faces mitigates against the

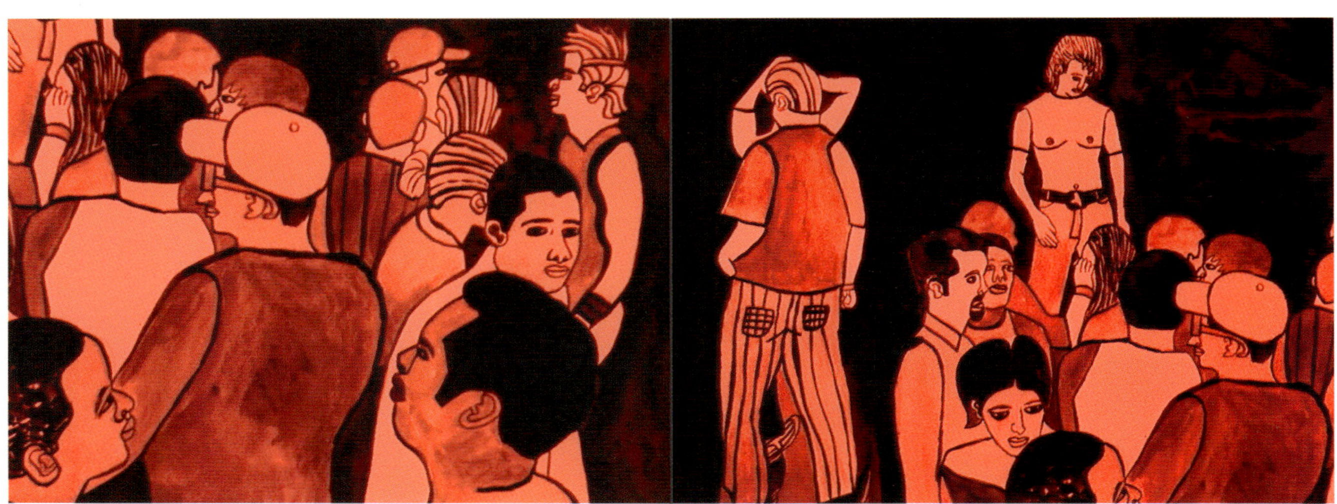

ominousness that such forms of surveillance often exude. All Benning's faces look
directly at the viewer and smile: crooked, wan, goofy, open, melancholic. They all
smile, as if we (the viewers) were a photographer commanding their performance. But
we're not a camera, and Sadie Benning isn't a photographer, so despite their enormous
size, the heads slip back into the register of painting. (It's a sign of how slippery and
odd they are that so far they have evoked for me ancient sculpture, parade balloons,
and photography.)

The history of the painted portrait is that of the ruling class: patrons, inserted
into manger scenes with the Virgin Mary and the infant Jesus during the Renaissance,
or enthroned in their homes and on display with their possessions by the nineteenth
century. "Look at me," they say. Indeed, the individual portrait is also an embodiment
of one of the most enduring ideas of western civilization: that we are individuals,
and that our personhood and rights stem from that inherent fact. The intensely
individuated quirkiness of these heads—despite the overwhelming similarity of their
enormous eyes, big broad noses, cherubic cheeks, and helmet-like hair—intimates
that they are portraits, likenesses of friends or colleagues of the artist. But they're not;
each one is an invention, a figment of Benning's imagination. One day when Sadie
and I were chatting she let it slip that she sometimes thinks of them as her imaginary
friends.

Benning has been able, in the past, to conjure extraordinary emotion through
her brute, almost childlike drawing line. In *Flat is Beautiful,* her 1998 video, all the
characters wear masks with black outlines of faces that appear part Matissean and part
simply rudimentary. Far from occluding the emotions of her subjects, these stiff paper
masks heighten the sense of alienation and existential loneliness felt by the characters
of the film. It's as if by masking the faces of her actors Benning allows the viewer
to look at the characters a little more baldly. The imaginary friends do look back,

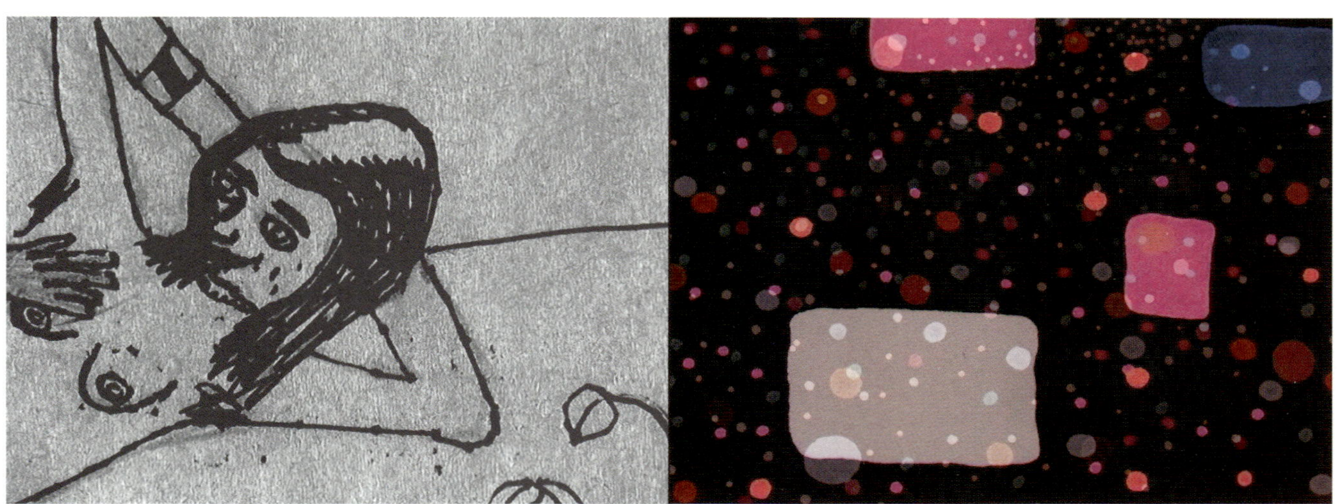

however, ruefully, knowingly, flirtatiously. They create a matrix of sorts, a web that we are caught in; they rearticulate the space we occupy. We are part of a group; we are no longer a solitary viewer. *We are not alone.*

Sadie Benning's work has a lot of queer content. Or maybe it's easier and more spot-on to say that Benning's work is queer. Certainly this is the case with *Flat is Beautiful*, a story about a young dyke navigating her way through the sexuality of the adults who surround her. But it's true of the imaginary friends as well. A room filled with the head paintings forms a kind of weird alternative universe, a place where people's identities float unhinged from their material bodies. This doesn't mean that they lack a gendered identity, but rather that the kind of ambiguity suggested in the faces registers a kind of porousness and openness toward the very concept of gendered identity. This is a definition of queerness that sees sexuality as a force of transformation and reorganization (of bodies, of identities, of pleasures and desires) as opposed to being a static and immutable fact. Amassed in a room together, Benning's imaginary friends form a kind of provisional community structured by a queer openness. In one of the few full-length pictures the words "I was born to[o] transform" appear above the figure's head.

The transformation of the imagined into the actual partakes of what political theorist Michael Warner has called a "counter public." For Warner a counter public does "more than represent the interests of gendered and sexualized persons in a public sphere. It can mediate the most private and intimate meanings of gender and sexuality."[1] I think the heads, with their whacked-out palette and ridiculous scale, their woeful and smiling eyes, and their refusal of the barbaric binarisms of gender, race, and sexuality, create a kind of space in which different (queer?) conversations are possible (like one between Emil Nolde and Beauford Delaney). Benning has invented a world and asked us to join in. As Warner says of specifically queer counter publics,

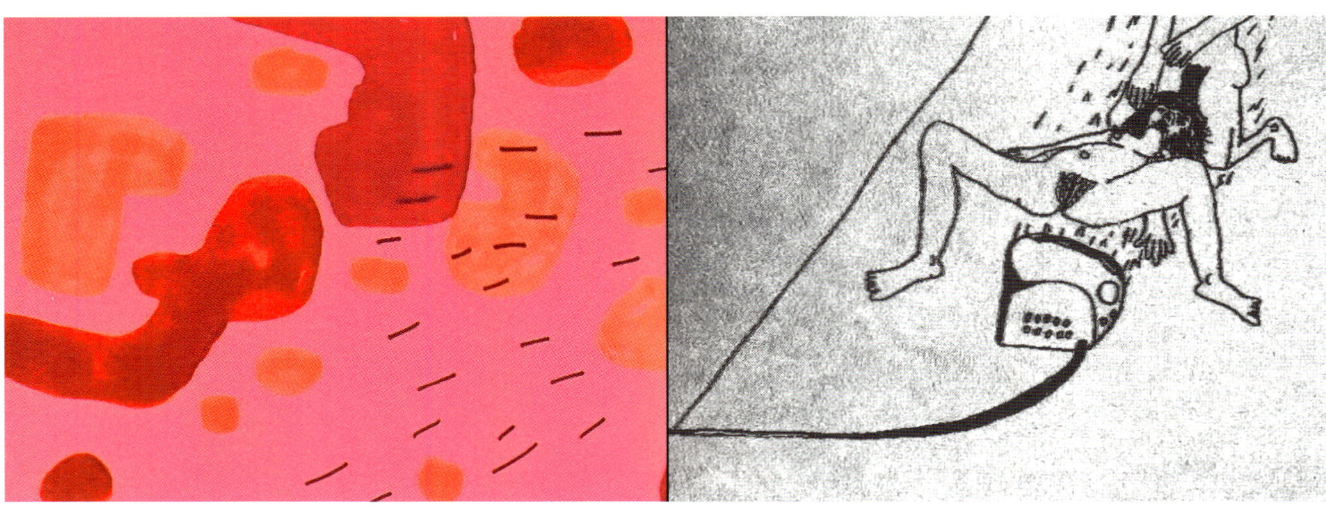

"Homosexuals can exist in isolation: but gay people or queers exist by virtue of the world they elaborate together."[2]

Play Pause follows a handful of anonymous protagonists through an unnamed city. Skyscrapers, public parks, and mass transit identify the space as consummately urban; the wide streets, flat, affectless light, and arching sense of space designate it as midwestern. The horror of our current political moment makes episodic appearances throughout the video: "No Receipt Available" spits out of an ATM as the Diebold brand name sneakily appears in the corner. The greed and avarice of the corporate world is emblazoned in newspaper headlines; security cameras at the airport X-ray our possessions. But the joy and beauty of the video comes in the scenes where queer people recast public space as their own—men cruising in a park, a night on the disco floor, and the scene at ZE BAR.

ZE BAR is a haven, a small patch of utopia, set off from the damaged politics of the city streets. It's not an unrealistic utopia, however. Irma Thomas sings about great loneliness and strife, her voice suffused with melancholy and loss. The characters in ZE BAR are the imaginary friends all grown up, and, having shed the ungainliness of youth, they are able to activate their desire and have created and are creating a space of intimacy. What's offered is not the intimacy of two people together, the logic of the couple, but the not-aloneness of the dance floor, the shared melody of the pop song, the pleasure of flirting with a stranger. It's the intimacy born of the knowing and acknowledging glances shared by queers on the street. *We are not alone.* It's the intimacy that comes from making a counter public, a series of spaces, activities, and gestures that affirm the transformational. It's the closeness that emerges from resisting the demands of adherence that come with ideas of community. (There are no "pride" marches in *Play Pause*, none of the heads wear rainbow coalition pins.) In the scenes in ZE BAR and on the dance floor public space is rearticulated as queer.

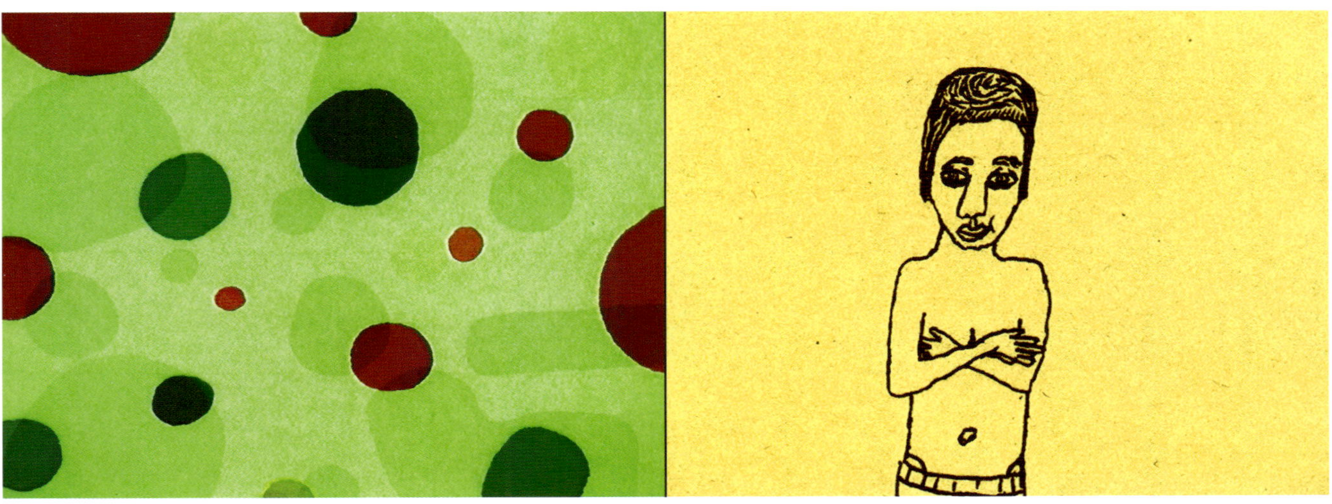

In the painted heads and *Play Pause* Benning offers us characters who are exploring modes of being that foster new possibilities for intimacy. This is why I think it's so important that the heads are not portraits of actual people. It's why the city in *Play Pause* is never named, because these are people and places and modes of being imagined by Benning, like the way we imagine our love into existence. (Love does not exist prior to us; we conjure it into being.) This is not an affirmation of what is but a testing of what can come to be. (It's not about pride, it's about imagining the possibility of change.) The end of *Play Pause* happens in an airport—the quintessential twenty-first-century space of loss and mourning, the ultimate signifier for our ever-more-transitory lives, a metaphor for the new extremes of our isolation from one another. This scene is the clearest distillation of *Play Pause*'s overall ambience. Here Benning suggests, affectively, that our current moment is structured by feelings of loss without nostalgia, shaped by experiences of tender desire that have no object, saturated with a melancholy acceptance of failure. Through its nuanced and moving soundtrack and its brave use of color, *Play Pause* instantiates the slightly numbed-out feelings of loss and desire that are so pervasive in our post-9/11 world. When her final characters start to make love, on the wings of an airplane in flight, we are immersed in the poignancy of the demand that our closest bonds of love are asked to stand the test of our increasingly nomadic and disjunctive lives. As clouds and blue sky move behind the fucking couple, like a rear screen projection, I think to myself, why not? Why not imagine impossible pleasures? Why not fathom new intimacies? Why not have imaginary friends?

[1] Michael Warner, *Publics and Counterpublics* (New York: Zone Books, 2002), p. 57.

[2] Ibid.

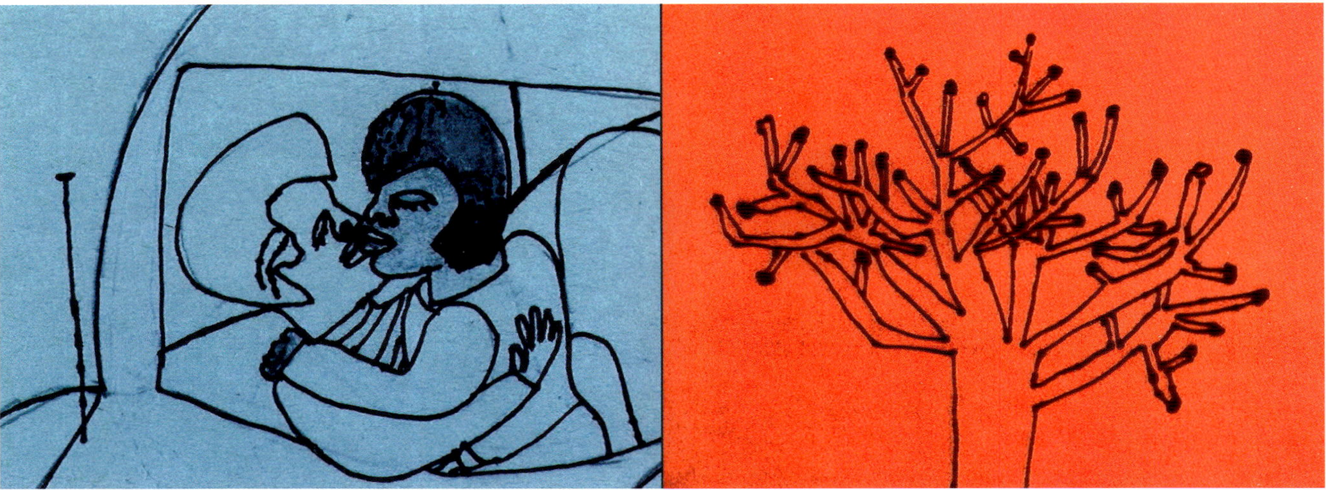

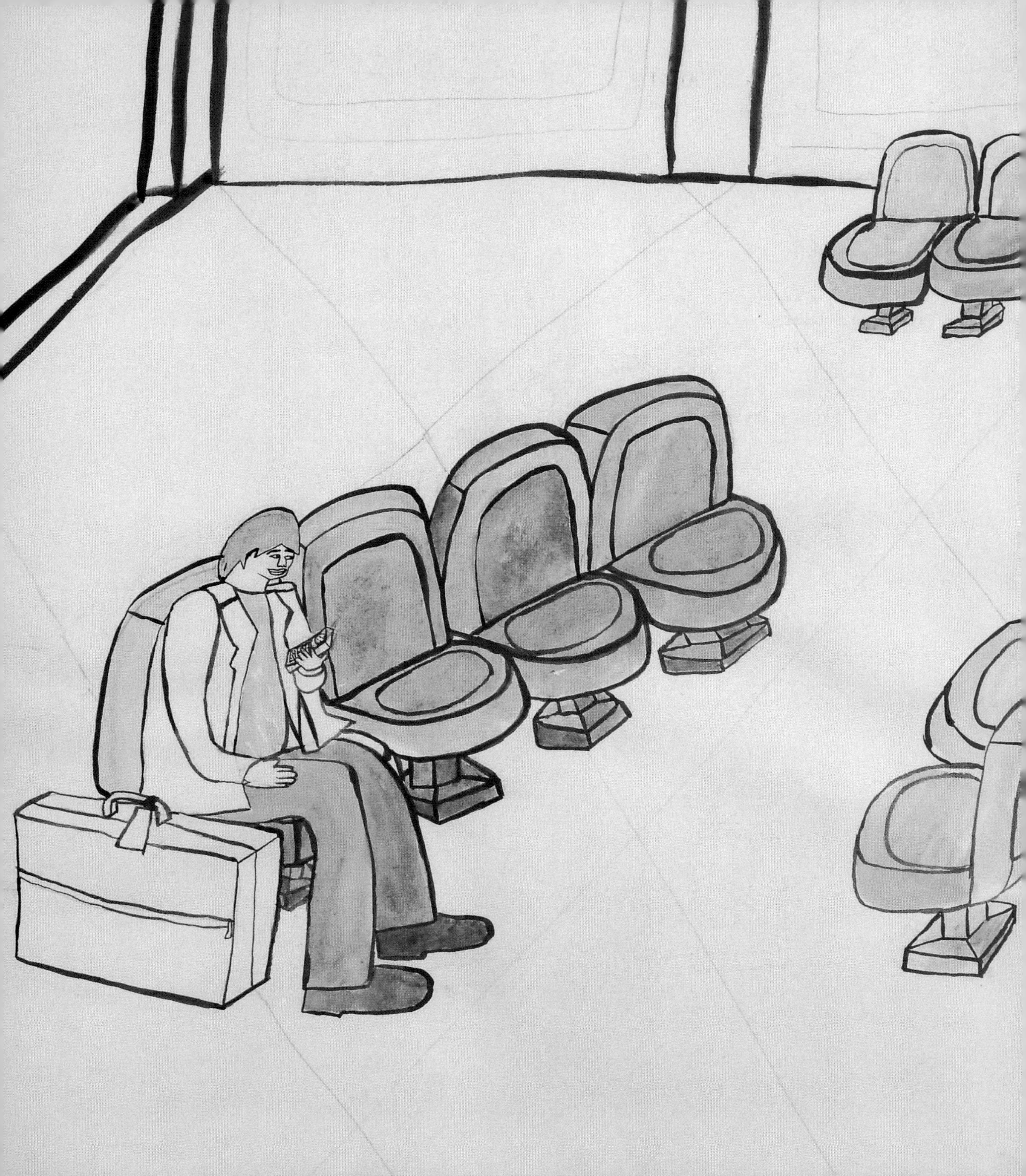

Aleksandar Hemon

We live in a country that is founded on, maintained by, and proud of its own lies and fantasies; in a culture obsessed with the bogus truthfulness of confessional autobiography and celebrity news; in an age in which it is possible to refer to "reality TV" without any irony. Our experience is so saturated with illusions—with *unreality*—that we crave whatever appears as real. Hence truth and reality are daily and cheaply produced in the patriotic factories of American capitalism, leading to an inflation of simulacra. That is to say, this might be a challenging time for art, which is—or at least ought to be—a mode of interaction with the real that depends on imagination. If the mind is to grasp the immensity of history and human experience, it must reach beyond an infinity of reproducible commodities sold under the guise of self-evident "reality," which always purports to be natural, artless, unimpeachably sovereign, continuously flowing forward. For "reality" to appear real, it is necessary to erase the seams and marks that expose it as produced. We have to believe that "reality TV" is but a window into the real, that everything is fixed as it is simply because it cannot be any other way.

All of which can only partly explain the unreal beauty and power of Sadie Benning's video work *Play Pause*. She has taken apart the edifice of "reality," assembled the chosen parts transformed into drawings, and constructed a reality that is governed by the rules of her impressive imagination.

The remnants of "reality" are visible and easily recognizable all over *Play Pause*.

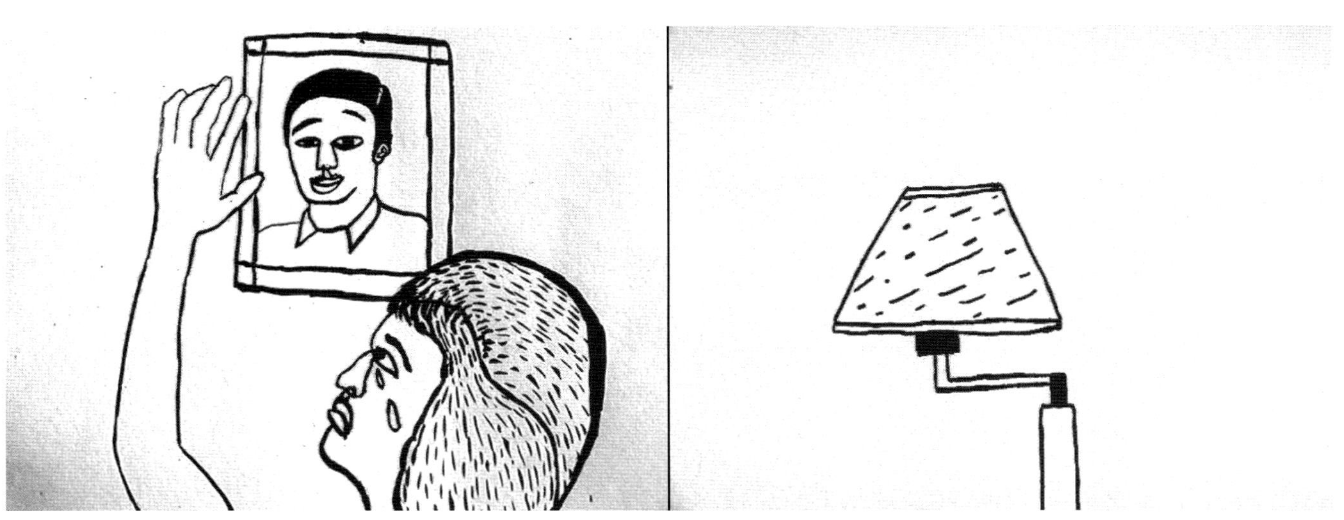

American power and the related national delusions are present in the images of soldiers with erected rifles and of patriots with their hands on their hearts, of American flags and of warnings saying "escalation level: orange & also yellow." But there are less dramatic particles of contemporary experience: ATM machines and banks; wrecking companies, warehouses, and dental offices; bars and cars and gas stations; signs offering "Breakfast Anytime" and the ecstasy of "Club Euphoria." There are businessmen and lovers and newspaper readers. There are buildings and highways and gay bars and airports. There are soccer players, corporate brands (allusively distorted), and TV sets, one of which blazes with "TOP 10 REALITY WEDDINGS!" There is sex, a lot of it. In short, there is a fullness of familiarity; we recognize life in an American city, and there is nothing we have not seen before. Yet one cannot escape the uncanny, marvelous feeling that we are seeing everything for the first time.

That is in fact the essence of Sadie Benning's art: seeing the familiar for the first time, whether through the lens of a Pixelvision camera in her early works or in *Play Pause*. For this to happen it is not enough just to dismantle the familiar or take apart what we perceive the world to be—any teenage punk band can do that. Rather, the audience needs to be seduced and coerced into the uncanniness of the familiar as it has never been experienced. And in doing so, *Play Pause* exhibits a dazzling array of Benning's transformative methods.

She quite literally redraws the world as seen in an American city (the immediate source for many of her drawings were photographs she had taken), whereby what she sees is simultaneously simplified and complicated by the seemingly child-like quality of her drawing style. Take the drawings in the sex scenes, which manage to appear both playful and cruel at the same time, due to the roughness of the line and the awkward-looking, off-balance, flat bodies.

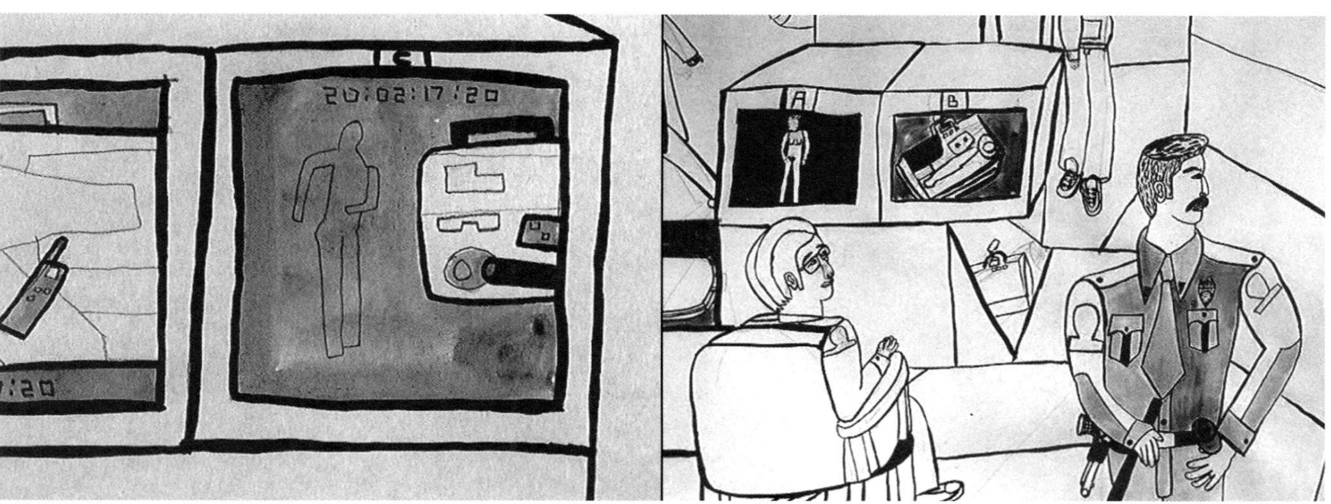

The most radical mode of transformation, however, comes from the two parallel screens on which Benning's reimagined, redrawn world unfolds. The literal duality of vision compels the viewer—with the two screens echoing her two eyes—to assemble a reality out of the disassembled "reality" while confronting the inescapable impossibility of ever succeeding. Gone is the counterfeit continuity of "the real," its sham seamlessness—for there is indeed a seam between the two screens, smack down the middle of our vision. The *seamfulness* is all the more stressed at the sublime, evanescent moments when the images on the two screens seem to unite.

Moreover, the dual vision allows Benning to take the concept of parallel montage to its logical extreme. In the conventional, movie use of parallel montage the images are connected by belonging to a forward-flowing temporal sequence, which merely falsifies simultaneity; in *Play Pause,* by contrast, images appear next to each other at the same time, thereby disrupting the forward flow—the images are welded to each other in the same moment and therefore cannot be reinserted into progressive temporality. By doubling the flow, Benning hits the pause button so we can pay attention to the world, so we can look at the conflicts and discontinuities that are inherent in our contemporary experience. Witness the parallel montage of a squirrel and a prettied-up woman; or an expressionless businessman on the right screen facing the sign for "Club Euphoria" on the left one. Or the sequence in which dark, mythical birds flow across the left screen, while on the right one there are images of sex—all of them are the sublimely beautiful, jarring moments of discontinuity.

In *Play Pause*, the world unfolds—*doubly*—before our eyes, not allowing us to assume the comfortable singular perspective, to settle into a lazy position on our metaphysical couch. We have to open both eyes, and each of them is seeing a different thing, the unity possible—albeit perishable—only in our heads. The depth of vision is destroyed, the flatness of the images doubled, restorable only by means of imagination.

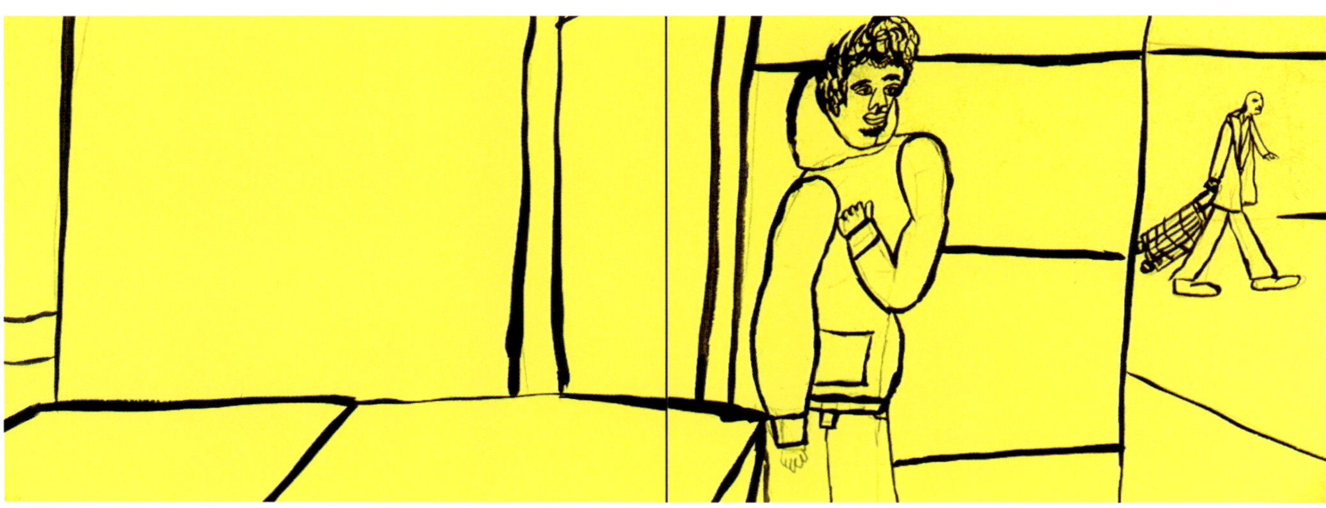

Benning—who has made a video called *Flat is Beautiful*—gives depth to her vision by flattening "reality," which lives by the delusion of singularity-cum-individuality of perspective. (Think of the handheld camera getting into the face of a reality-show participant, or deep-&-cheap individualistic suffering in confessional memoirs.) When on one of the screens the images are flowing, while the other shows a static drawing, Benning is bravely skimming the surface, forcing us to confront the two dimensions before we dive into the false depths of the third one. In *Play Pause* the world is *surfaced* so it can surface.

What we get in return for the lost third dimension is not only twice as much two-dimensionality but plenty of sound as well. The soundtrack of the flat double-vision consists not only of the incidental music, written and performed by Benning herself, but also of found city sounds she has recorded. The effect of hearing the sound of construction at the very beginning, or birds twittering, while you are looking at the parallel flow of drawings, is a sense that there is far more life, world, reality behind the two screens. Although "reality" is always complete (there is nothing beyond it, except, perhaps, some sort of spiritual fantasy park, just a reality show of a different order), human reality is always incomplete, if for no other reason than because we cannot extend ourselves—except by means of imagination—into others. The sounds, familiar as they are, come from the depths of the beautiful Benning world, across whose surface we are moving.

A lot has been made of Benning's lesbian identity, and her work is frequently qualified as autobiographical—her main subject being, one critic wrote, herself. But labeling a work of art—let alone the entire opus of an artist—as autobiographical dangerously approaches reducing it to a mere concealed, if self-indulgent, confession. The autobiographical-interpretative approach treats art as a form of therapy; it reduces it to an uncomplicated narrative of self-fulfillment and redemption, whereby the

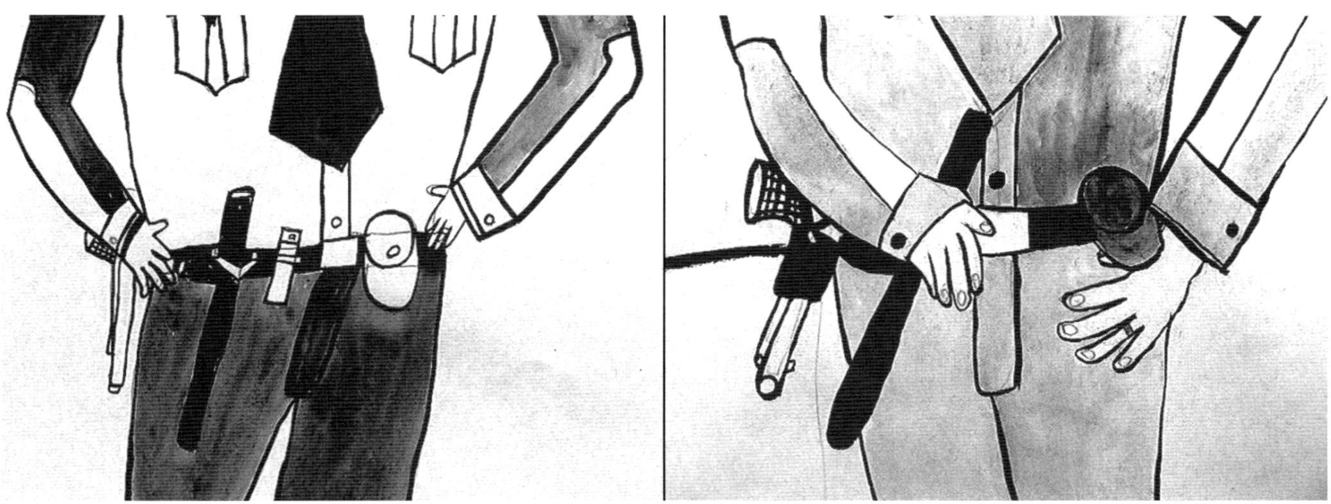

audience might—or might not—voyeuristically participate in the titillating rituals of self-realization. Such interpretations turn art into nothing but an interesting way to talk about oneself.

So let me venture to say that autobiographical art is always to some extent a contradiction in terms. There is a fundamental difference between the personal and the autobiographical. While the main subject of autobiographical art is the self of the artist, the subject of personal art is the world (as an ontological entity) in which that self is rooted and operates. Autobiographical art is confessional; personal art is relational. The essence of autobiographical art is the hard core of the self, the metaphysical ground zero, from which all others are banished. Personal art expands toward other human beings until a network of connections is established. Autobiographical art is all but vacant; personal art is a space in which the presence of others is necessary.

Benning's art—from her earliest Pixelvision works shot in her bedroom, to *Play Pause*, her most mature and advanced work to date—has always been about this personal space, about the ways she relates to the world and its ineluctable materiality. Her art is about what she sees, about the transformative possibilities of her presence in the world as we share it.

What is remarkable about *Play Pause* is not just its formal brilliance and the intense beauty of Benning's vision, but also an extraordinary warmth (often banished from postmodern and contemporary art), which doubtless comes from her interest in people. Such interest is in the ideological space of "reality" often deflected toward effigies that stand in for human beings and communities: celebrities, athletes, patriotic politicians and presidents, national/nationalistic governments and TV wars, etc. So when an artist of Benning's talent succeeds in salvaging enough "reality" debris to construct a personal space in which she can invite others to confront and experience the world, we have a reason to celebrate. And the reason is called *Play Pause*.

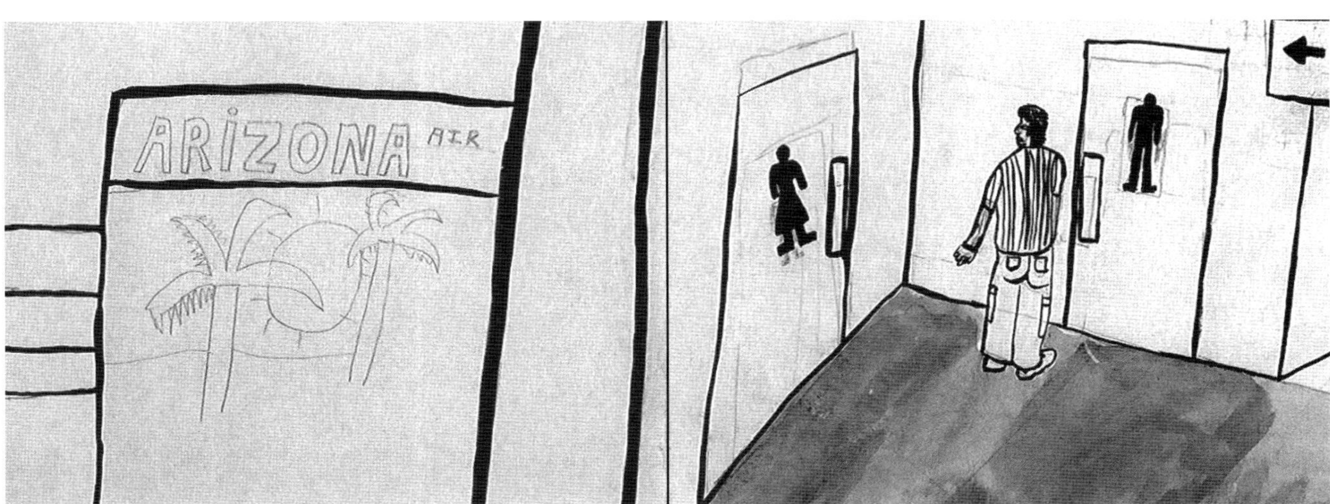

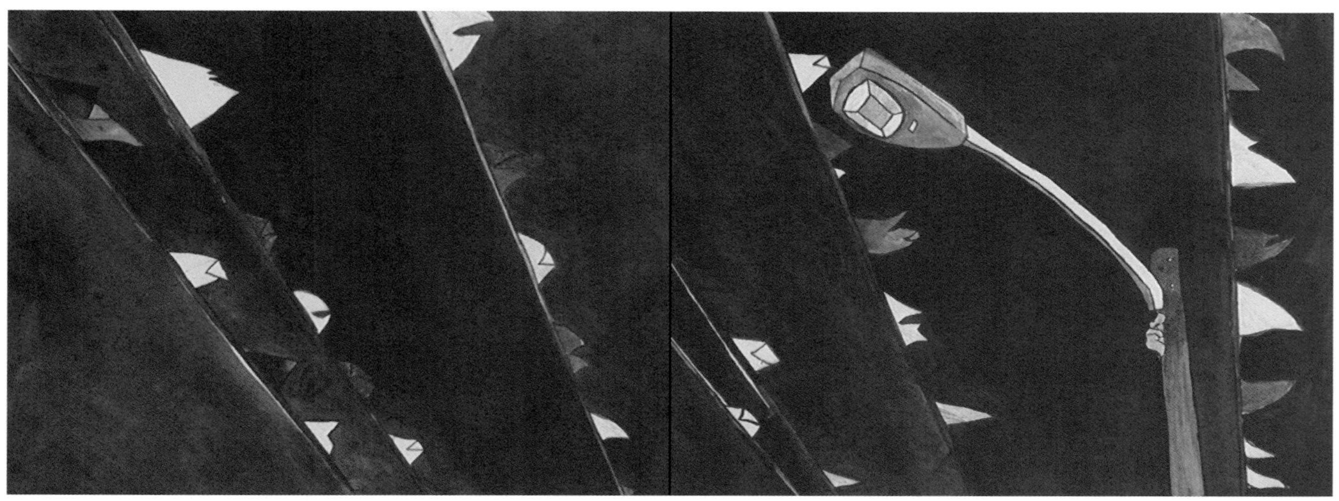

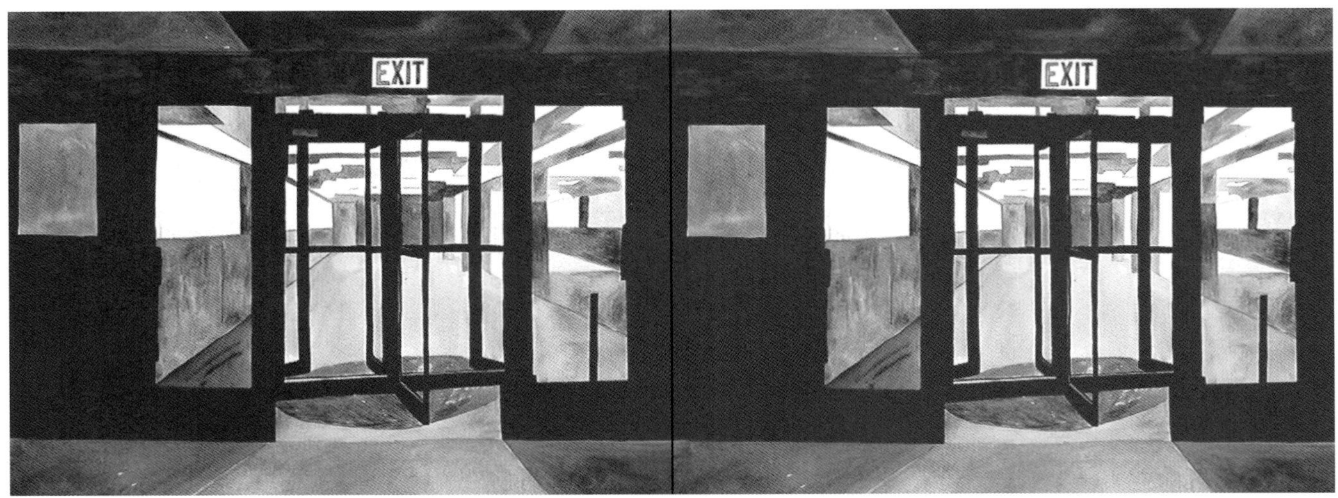

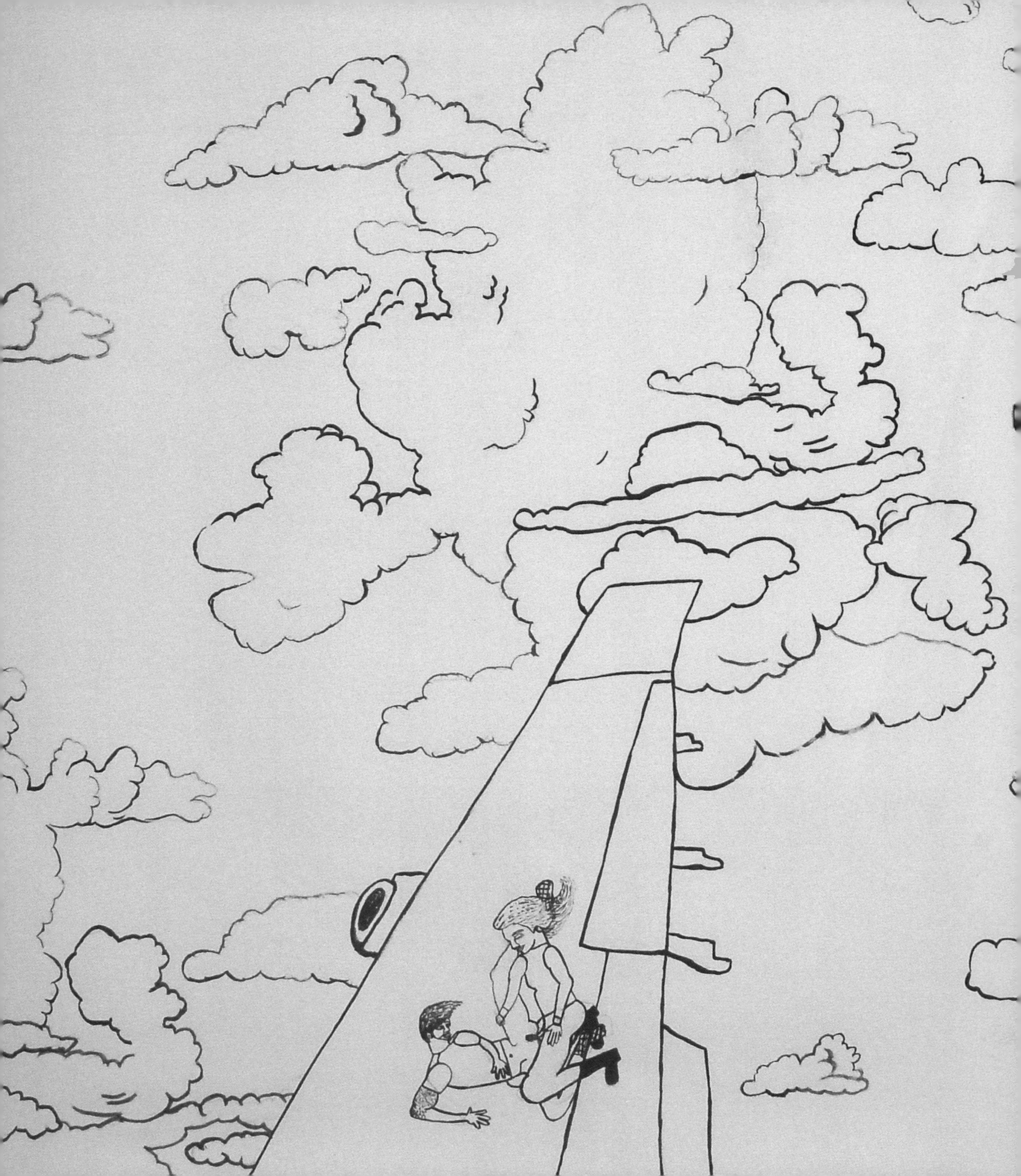

PAINTINGS

all night long, all night, 2001
Flashe paint on paper
86 x 38 in.
(p. 55)

billie golfing, 2001
Flashe paint on paper
99 x 72 in.
(p. 49)

karen, 2001
Flashe paint on paper
74 x 99 in.
(p. 52)

untitled, 2001
Flashe paint on canvas
81 x 66 in.
(p. 43)

we got the beat, 2001
Flashe paint on paper
96 x 72 in.
(p. ii, detail, and p. 48)

I'm going surfing, really surfing, 2002
Flashe paint on paper
96 x 74 in.
(p. 47)

kissing couple, 2002
Flashe paint on canvas
89 x 69 in.
(p. 59)

see you later, 2002
Flashe paint on paper
92 x 74 in.
(p. 50)

vivian in a priest costume, 2002
Flashe paint on paper
98 x 74 in.
(p. 51)

beauty b, 2003
Flashe paint on canvas
85 x 68 in.
(p. 56)

Chicago, March 20, 2003, 2003
Flashe paint on paper
95 x 40 in.
(p. 44)

waiting, 2003
Flashe paint on paper
79 x 73 in.
(p. 45)

I was born to transform, 2004
Flashe paint on paper
90 x 39 in.
(p. 54)

lack of interest, 2004
Flashe paint on paper
89 x 61 in.
(p. 46)

lady in a purple beret, 2004
Flashe paint on paper
77 x 61 in.
(p. 53)

blue lips, looking, 2006
Flashe paint on canvas
92 x 81 in.
(p. 57)

VIDEO

Play Pause, 2006
Two-channel projection from hard drive
6 x 8 ft., each channel
Running time: 29 mins., 22 secs.
(stills from *Play Pause* are reproduced
in pairs throughout the catalogue)

ALL WORKS ARE COURTESY OF THE ARTIST. IN DIMENSIONS, HEIGHT PRECEDES WIDTH.

Sadie Benning was born in Madison, Wisconsin, in 1973 and grew up in Milwaukee. She started making videos as a teenager with a Fisher Price Pixelvision camera and received her M.F.A. from Bard College in 1997. Her videos have been exhibited internationally in film festivals, museums, galleries, and universities since 1990 with select solo screenings at the Museum of Modern Art, Film Society of Lincoln Center, Walker Art Center, Centre Georges Pompidou, Harvard University, and Hallwalls Contemporary Arts Center, among other venues. The Wexner Center has screened her videos on several occasions, including a retrospective series curated by Bill Horrigan in 2004. Her video work is in many permanent collections, including those of the Museum of Modern Art and the Walker Art Center, and has been included in the following exhibitions: Whitney Biennial (1993 and 2000); *Building Identities*, Tate Modern (2004); *Remembrance and the Moving Image*, Australian Centre for the Moving Image (2003); *Video Viewpoints*, Museum of Modern Art (2002); *American Century*, Whitney Museum of American Art (2000); *Love's Body*, Tokyo Museum of Photography (1999); *Scream and Scream Again: Film in Art*, Museum of Modern Art Oxford (1996–97); and Venice Biennale (1993).

Benning has exhibited her paintings in group shows at Threadwaxing Space (1998) and Orchard (2006). She is a former member and cofounder, with Kathleen Hanna and Johanna Fateman, of the music group Le Tigre. She has received grants and fellowships from, among others, Guggenheim Foundation, Andrea Frank Foundation, National Endowment for the Arts, and the Rockefeller Foundation. Awards include the Wexner Center Residency Award in media arts, National Alliance for Media Arts & Culture Merit Award, Grande Videokunst Prize, and the Los Angeles Film Critics Circle Award. Since 1992 her videos have been distributed by the Video Data Bank in Chicago.

VIDEOGRAPHY

Me & Rubyfruit, 1989
Black and white video / Pixelvision, 5 mins., 30 secs.

A New Year, 1989
Black and white video / Pixelvision, 6 mins.

Living Inside, 1989
Black and white video / Pixelvision, 4 mins.

If Every Girl Had a Diary, 1990
Black and white video / Pixelvision, 9 mins.

Welcome to Normal, 1990
Color video / Hi 8, 20 mins.

Jollies, 1990
Black and white video / Pixelvision, 11 mins.

A Place Called Lovely, 1991
Black and white video / Pixelvision, 15 mins.

It Wasn't Love, 1992
Black and white video / Pixelvision, 20 mins.

Girl Power, 1992
Black and white video / Pixelvision, 15 mins.

The Judy Spots, 1995
Color video / 16 mm film, 12 mins., 30 secs.

German Song, 1995
Black and white video / Super 8 film, 6 mins.

Flat is Beautiful, 1998
Black and white video / Pixelvision, 16 mm and Super 8 film, 56 mins.

Aerobicide, 1999
Color digital video, 5 mins.
Codirected with Kathleen Hanna.

The Baby, 2003
Installation, color digital video / drawings on paper, 5 mins., 39 secs.

One Liner, 2003
Installation, black and white video / Pixelvision, 5 mins., 7 secs.

Play Pause, 2006
Two-channel projection from hard drive, color digital video / drawings on paper, 29 mins., 22 secs.

Aleksandar Hemon was born in Sarajevo, Bosnia-Herzegovina, and graduated from the University of Sarajevo with a degree in literature in 1990. He arrived in Chicago in 1992 for what was to be a short visit but found himself stranded by the escalating conflict in Bosnia-Herzegovina. Since 1999 his stories in English have been published in the *New Yorker*, *Esquire*, *Granta*, and *Ploughshares* and collected in the 1999 and 2000 editions of *The Best American Short Stories*. His books include *The Question of Bruno*, a collection of stories, and *Nowhere Man*, a novel.

Jennifer Lange has been associate curator of media arts at the Wexner Center since 2001. She curates the Art & Technology residency program, as well as monthly programs of short video work for The Box video exhibition space. Through the residency program, she has supported projects by Deborah Stratman, Phil Collins, Sowon Kwon, and Josiah McElheny, among others. She has also served as a judge for the *Journal of Short Film*, a quarterly DVD publication. From 1999 to 2001 she worked at Donald Young Gallery in Chicago, where she also earned an M.A. from the School of the Art Institute of Chicago.

Helen Molesworth is chief curator of exhibitions at the Wexner Center, where her recent exhibitions have included *Twice Untitled and Other Pictures (looking back)* (2006), a collection of old and new work by artist Louise Lawler, and *Part Object Part Sculpture* (2005), which charted a genealogy of transatlantic sculpture produced in the wake of Marcel Duchamp's erotic objects and his handmade readymades of the 1960s. From 2000 to 2003 she was the curator of contemporary art at The Baltimore Museum of Art. Her writing has appeared in publications such as *Artforum*, *Art Journal, Documents*, and *October*, as well as in numerous exhibition catalogues.

Eileen Myles has written thousands of poems since she gave her first reading at CBGB's in 1974. A prominent figure in the East Village art and music scene, she was artistic director of St. Mark's Poetry Project (1984–86) and wrote, acted in, and directed plays at St. Mark's and PS 122. She has read to audiences at colleges, performance spaces, and bookstores across America as well as in Europe, Iceland, and Russia and toured with Sister Spit's Ramblin' Road Show in 1997. Her books include *Skies: New Poems*, *Cool for You*, and *Chelsea Girls*. She's a frequent contributor to *Bookforum, Art in America,* the *Village Voice*, the *Nation*, and *Open City*, and she's blogging weekly at *openfordesign.msn.com*. A professor of literature at the University of California, San Diego, she just completed a novel titled *The Inferno*. *Sorry, Tree* (poems) will be published in April 2007.

Solveig Nelson collaborated with Sadie Benning on the narrative and editing of *Play Pause*. For the past eight years she has worked in Chicago as a literary programmer, bookseller, and editor. She is the former director of public programs at the Seminary Co-op Bookstores and the fiction editor at *The Baffler*.

Amy Sillman is a painter who lives and works in New York. Recent exhibitions of her work include solo shows at Sikkema Jenkins & Co. in New York City and Susanne Vielmetter LA Projects in Los Angeles, and group shows such as the 2004 Whitney Biennial, *The Triumph of Painting* at the Saatchi Gallery in London, and the Wexner Center exhibition *Landscape Confection*, which traveled to the Contemporary Arts Museum, Houston, and the Orange County Museum of Art.

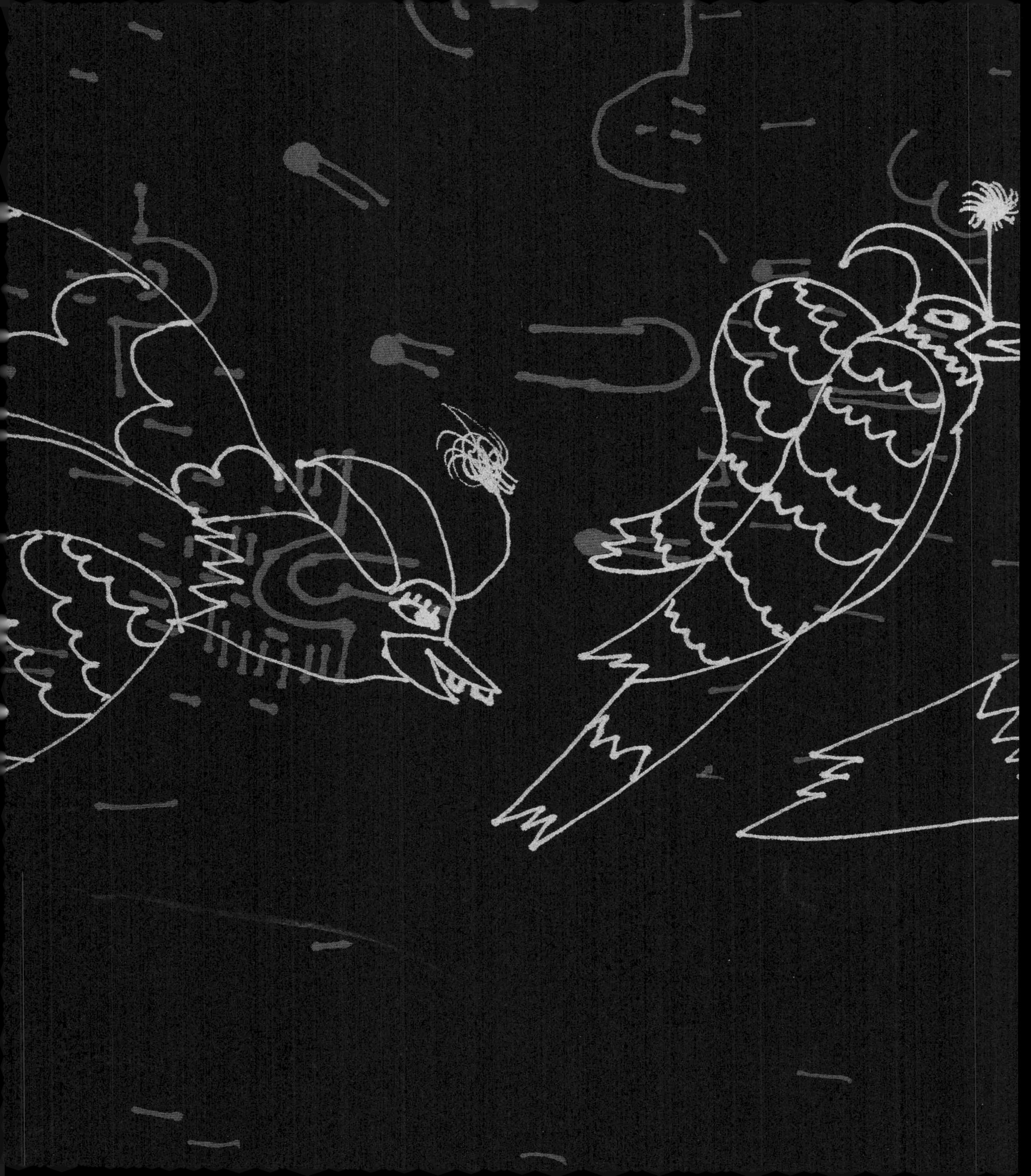